Date Due

Leaders in Norway

and Other Essays

Frontispiece   *The Eidsvold Congress*   Painted by Oscar Wergeland

(The man in the open door is Nicolai Wergeland. Ed.)

Leaders in Norway
and Other Essays

AGNES MATHILDE WERGELAND
(Late Professor of History, University of Wyoming)

Edited and arranged by
KATHARINE MERRILL

Essay Index Reprint Series

BOOKS FOR LIBRARIES PRESS, INC.
FREEPORT, NEW YORK

First published 1916
Reprinted 1966

81710

Printed In The United States of America

PREFACE

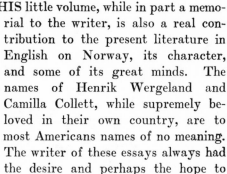

THIS little volume, while in part a memorial to the writer, is also a real contribution to the present literature in English on Norway, its character, and some of its great minds. The names of Henrik Wergeland and Camilla Collett, while supremely beloved in their own country, are to most Americans names of no meaning. The writer of these essays always had the desire and perhaps the hope to make better known to the world the particular characteristics and accomplishment of her beloved fatherland. Had opportunity been granted her to fulfill that desire, any lacks that may be felt in the present work, compiled as it has been merely from disconnected publications and miscellaneous papers, would have been abundantly supplied from the wealth of knowledge and loving familiarity which she carried in her heart and memory.

Of those who have aided in this undertaking, the most devoted thanks are due to Miss Maren Michelet, of Minneapolis, one of the leaders in the teaching of Norse in this country, who has generously furnished translations and historical and literary information which otherwise to a person unacquainted with Norse would have been practically inaccessible.

Cordial acknowledgment is also made to the publishers of *The Dial*, *The North American Review*, *Symra*, and other English and Norse periodicals for permission to reprint some of the articles here included.

TABLE OF CONTENTS

TO the memory of a friend who had more than one string to her lute and who through many vicissitudes always remained true to her individuality, this book is dedicated by those who most cherish the abiding influence of her rich friendship.

THE PRIMITIVE NORSEMAN

I F we scan the old sagas to learn the dominating traits of the race that produced them, we find as one leading characteristic a strong sense of individual value, of respect for self. This was expressed not only outwardly in a proud, well-poised bearing but also inwardly. There was no bowing to a superior merely because he was above, no kneeling in the dust or kissing the hem of his garment because it was the fashion to do so as a servile habit, but only because inner recognition of his actual worth allowed it. The homage done was real. There was a plain honesty in those Northern Teutons that stood them in good stead, for it prevented them from being enslaved during the time when all the rest of Europe was under the yoke.

Closely related to this vigorous self-respect was the chastity in the spirit of the race. The brutality of barbarous tribes cannot, of course, be gainsaid; but there are incidents and remarks in the old poems that indicate a natural proud reserve and a certain restraint upon the feelings which even today distinguish the Scandinavian nations from most others. It is not so much a product of reflection as an innate dislike of excess. This emotional reserve indicates even today—not that they have no feeling—but that they check themselves through the fear of going too far if they take all possible freedom. This quality is a source of moral fortitude in the race.

Another quality quite as characteristic as the two mentioned is faithfulness. The old sagas show that an individual might resist a long time, trying to maintain his absolute independence. But when he once became attached, either by law or by affection, he was faithful with an equally absolute faithfulness. What the Germans meant by the keeping of servant's faith toward the master—the "treu und glaube" of feudal life, was eminently characteristic of relationship in the entire Germanic world. It was upon the individual's "treu und glaube" more than upon any other thing that the whole society, feudal relations and all, rested. The old sagas speak of instance after instance of a man's pledging his word and in every case living up to it. Friends mix drops of their blood in order to bind each other forever as with a natural tie; the nobleman sacrifices all for his lord, the warrior for his king; the betrothed keeps his troth even when a better marriage is offered him and when there is nothing but his word to bind him.

Yet another striking trait found in the heroes and heroines of northern sagas is simplicity of feeling, oneness of purpose, a stability of character that did not yield to excruciating doubts or to complicated analysis of motives such as belong to our modern life. These old heroes and heroines seem hewn in rock, like mountains with meadows at their feet and snow on their heads—and yet, like the rock of which they were hewn, they hid fire in their bosom. Passion was there and heat, wild hatred, anguish and love slowly working, silently subdued but unexpectedly bursting forth like

flame from an impassive volcano that suddenly illumi-
nates everything with its sombre glow. Remember
Brynhild, who preferred to see Sigurd dead rather
than alive with another woman.

Such incidents as this manifest the dramatic, intense
quality of Northern poetry and likewise of the mythology. In the old Germanic lore of the gods there is
no licentious Zeus nor lovesick Aphrodite. Odin, father
of the gods, has given one of his eyes in exchange for
wisdom. His desire is for that. He is indeed a majestic, awe-inspiring figure of the first order; the mystery
of all things seems to hide under the shadow of his
great gray mantle and the broad hat that shades his
brow. Jupiter, whose eyebrows shake the world, seems
weak and soft beside him. And Thor and Tyr, Balder
and Ydun—how much more force and majesty are in
them than in the Greek deities of somewhat the same
nature.

Thus the early Norsemen possessed certain sympathetic qualities, certain large virtues which just because of their simplicity and genuineness create an impression of greatness; a greatness that the far more
polished, complicated character of the civilized man of
that time or of man today does not produce. The
civilized man seems almost artificial compared with
these simple, true individuals whom he may be inclined
to despise; and yet in some broad noble ways he is not
able to surpass them.

[3]

THE AWAKENING OF NORWAY

ARLY in the middle ages Norway presented an interesting picture of great national force and activity. The country contained perhaps less than a million inhabitants and only one third of the present area was cultivated. On the coast alone was a somewhat dense population, and even that was mostly scattered into separate homesteads, since there were very few towns. Yet the nation had remarkable vigor and vitality. Evidence of this is found in the emigrations of the time—for example, the populating of Iceland and the Scotch islands; also in the conquests of Ireland and Normandy. In later centuries journeys were made, too, to such distant points as Palestine and Constantinople and the coast of the western continent. To the intellectual life of those ages Norway contributed its sagas and poems, its mythology, and last, but not least, one of the most interesting collections of laws in existence. All these, moreover, were recorded in the national language; and this at a time when in the Frankish empire and long afterwards Latin was the only tongue used for literary purposes or even for law practice. These manifestations prove that Norway was not intellectually or politically isolated and barbaric, but lead us rather to see that it was prominent and a country of peculiar significance within in the Germanic world.

But the later mediæval time shows a change. From the ninth to the thirteenth century, five hundred years, Norway was consumed by internal wars. They may not have been very extensive or have made much difference in the general life of the people. But they kept the country in constant excitement, and slowly though surely sapped its strength, leaving it finally exhausted and paralytic.

Norway started in history as one of the most aristocratic countries on record. Not only was there a very high nobility, consisting of previous territorial earls who had submitted their possessions to a victorious king while retaining their prestige and rank as magnates, but, besides, every small owner of allodial lands was by virtue of those very possessions and his old free lineage a nobleman likewise. The word peasant meant nothing derogatory, as in other countries. Rather, it was a title of consequence and a pride to its owner. Those free peasants—whose descendants in many instances maintain today the same aristocratic bearing as their ancestors a thousand years ago—were the people proper, the people that met at the court of the hundred, the people that pleaded causes, passed judgments, accepted the newly elected king or rejected him, and ruled the land according to old custom and with a degree of popular freedom such as had been the idea of the Germanic race from the very first.

When the period of struggle began, the effort of the monarchy was, first, to fight the higher aristocracy, which tried to divert the royal power to its own side;

and second, to reduce the political activity of the free peasantry to local matters only. This conflict filled the greater part of the centuries following the ninth. The monarchy, represented by many brilliant warriors and rulers, steadily increased in prestige. The struggling aristocracy received the greatest blow in the twelfth century when they tried to raise from their own circle a pretender to the vacant throne and were defeated. A new family was established, that of Sverre, whom some considered a usurper while others thought he claimed only his right as a descendant of the old family.

This age-long bloody struggle exhausted the higher aristocracy and made the lower obedient subjects to a royal power almost absolute. For though this power was seemingly in strict conformity to the laws of the country, yet it held in its hand complete political supremacy. The old Germanic notion that all sons of a king should be considered heirs to the throne—which had hitherto prevailed in Norway—had been one of the chief causes of internal strife, because it tempted the aristocracy to divide their support. Now, however, this was set aside for the rule that only the oldest legitimate son could be king. And so strong and undisputed grew the kingly authority, that in spite of the previous order of succession, natural to the country and used in private affairs, the idea of strict legitimate primogeniture became, for the throne, almost an axiom among the Norwegian people. As time passed, the king to such an extent concentrated all power in

[6]

his person and was so much regarded as the real source of government and law, that not even the French nation after the days of Louis XIV was less able to rule itself and choose a representative government from its own body politic than was the Norwegian after the old royal family had died out and the question arose of where to seek a successor. Then came the period of extreme impotency, even degradation, when the first union with Sweden was formed; and later the equally unfortunate relation to Denmark. Norway was like a ship without a rudder, a prey to every wind and wave.

The cause of these deplorable events can be sought nowhere but in the political conditions within the country itself. The rapid disappearance of its aristocracy, the absence of leaders among the free peasants and their lack of broad political training such as they had possessed in earlier times, the financial exhaustion of the nation, and finally even the very law-abiding spirit of the people themselves—these things caused them to cling with almost contemptible weakness to the letter of the law, and prevented them from seeing that the emergencies of the times demanded immediate action, even though contrary to the prescriptions of previous years.

Such paralysis in countries once active is nothing new but is always regrettable. The national misfortunes in Norway began when in the fourteenth century Haakon the Fifth had no possible heir but a daughter. Only male heirs were recognized by law. To save the country from internal war, Haakon had changed the

order of succession so that the son of his daughter
should inherit the throne. This daughter, Princess
Ingeborg, had married a Swedish prince who at the
time had no expectation of inheriting the throne of his
own country and who was expected to be to the princess
only a prince consort or even less, because she herself
could never be more than regent for her son. This
son, however, by a strange trick of fortune, became the
king of both countries. Thus began one of the many
so-called personal unions of Sweden and Norway. The
union was liked even less by Norway than by Sweden,
for although it was the Norwegian king who became
ruler of both, yet Norway found itself slighted and
neglected. The two nations were separated again when
the king's sons grew up and the elder became his col-
league in Sweden (again a slight to Norway), while the
younger became an associate and finally an independent king in Norway itself. So far so good. But a new
series of complications arose when this young Norwegian king married the only heir to the Danish throne,
the Princess Margrete—their son being thus the future
ruler of both Norway and Denmark. This son, however, as well as his father, died. Then appeared the
first astonishing instance of the incapacity of the Norwegian people to take care of their own interests. The
Norwegian state council weakly accepted as their mistress the Danish Queen Margrete. The fact that she
had been regent of her son was her only possible claim
to a throne from which women had for centuries been
excluded by law. On the part of the council it was

only a desperate attempt to bridge over a time of inter-regnum till a new king could be elected. To elect a king from among the aristocracy does not seem to have occurred to the nation. The Danish princess and queen soon united to her double scepter the third country also. Thus came about the first instance of the so-called Kalmar union—a union that might have worked much good if the nations had not for centuries been on somewhat hostile terms.

If Queen Margrete may be credited with the earliest conception of a united northern empire, the idea of which has occupied many later minds, she at least lacked the political wisdom to see that what is near but not dear will have to be joined together by force of arms or be led to approach by steps likely to be but slow. Margrete, however, accomplished little toward such an approach. In fact, she created antagonism by making the other two countries feel neglected and used merely as footstools for Danish glory. The Norwegians particularly had no reason to be elated over their choice of mistress, and yet they seem not to have made any particular protest. Their submission to royal authority even led them to accept and crown as their lawful king the successor Margrete chose for herself, namely, a German prince in no way connected with the royal Norwegian family. This prince later became the king of Denmark and Sweden as well. But though he embraced the idea of a Northern empire as eagerly as his predecessor, he saw as little as she the natural difficulties in carrying out the plan and

[9]

fought in vain the separatist tendencies in each of his countries. The union gradually became an object of hatred to all of them. Only Denmark as the superior country derived some benefit from it and was longest in favor of it. The king, however, soon came into conflict with the Danish and Swedish aristocracies, which were much more aggressive than the Norwegian. Both countries declared him deposed. Norway alone clung to the cause of the king who had never cared, even after his deposition, to acknowledge this faithfulness or to set his foot in the country. Denmark chose a new king, and he by common consent soon became the Swedish monarch. Presently in the same way he added Norway to his possessions, that country still remaining incapable of initiative. Thus came a repetition of the much detested Kalmar union.

This king, however, died not long afterwards without leaving heirs; and then the Norwegians were met by the most difficult dilemma that had confronted them. Sweden chose a king from the nation itself, one of its own noblemen; thus establishing its independence and national career. Norway seems to have seen no such possibility. The Danes, instead of following the example of the Swedes, again chose a German prince, though he had not the slightest connection with the Danish royal house. By a hurried journey to Norway, this new king, whose name was Kriestiern of Oldenburg, succeeded without difficulty in being elected king of Norway as well—that being the second instance of Dano-Norwegian union based upon a king in common.

Kings of the Oldenburg house from then on for four hundred years remained the rulers of both countries —it is safe to say not to the advantage of either. The grandson of Kriestiern I once more united all three countries under his scepter. But his tryannical rule alienated Sweden forever from friendly relation to the Danish monarchy. He, too, was deposed, and although Norway, as in the previous case, remained longest faithful to him, he disregarded this and concentrated all his energies on the overcoming of his enemies in Denmark. He made a voyage to southern Norway and from there entered Denmark; but was met with treacherous promises, captured under false pretenses and remained in prison for twenty-three years. Thus ended this inglorious drama—the point of interest being the treatment that the submissive Norway received from the self-seeking holders of her vacant throne.

Further detail is unnecessary concerning this ignominious decay of a once active state. Suffice it to say that the lethargy was taken advantage of by the Danes, who thus at small cost united with their own country another which seemed incapable of resisting any aggression. The Danes in the period of union utilized Norway as if it had been a conquered province. The Norwegians furnished the Danish army with soldiers and the Danish fleet with sailors. Norway contributed twice or three times as much to the Danish treasury as Denmark paid out for Norwegian defense. Danish farmers had a monopoly in selling grain to Norwegian provinces. The castles of Norway were commanded by Danish noblemen, the administrators were mostly Danes, even the language was called Danish, and the existence of Norway as a separate kingdom was calmly and completely ignored. No country conquered by an enemy could be more wholly absorbed; and no country that was not suffering from absolute prostration could endure such loss of natural rights.

Such was the result of the earlier war between the aristocracy and the monarchy and the absorption of all political power by the king. Instead of an aristocratic society, the Norwegian had become democratic; but it was not a democracy with any capacity for political action. Having no longer natural leaders, and having lost the sense of self-leadership, the nation easily became the prey of greed and selfish neglect.

And yet in spite of all that weak sufferance, and even in the days of Norway's closest relation to Denmark when the feeling of nationality was least awake, the sense of being a separate nation never left the heart of the people. The mountaineer maintains his individuality far longer than the inhabitant of the plain. Norwegians who rose to prominent recognition and rank within the Danish state never forgot that they were of Norwegian origin. They were proud of the fact, and this pride and self-esteem gave them a peculiar independent bearing that reflected glory upon the country from which they came. Even as early as the sixteenth century, under the influence of the general European humanistic movement, the old sagas telling the exploits of the valiant earls and kings of former days had been translated and read with the greatest interest throughout the country. That heroic past was by no means disregarded. Men looked back with pride and pleasure to those ages when Norway had stood in the front rank among the northern nations.

Another event that wakened patriotic sentiment was the need and successful outcome of Norway's self-defense against Charles XII of Sweden. Denmark, in spite of her eagerness to absorb Norway, was not in the habit of doing much to protect this valuable aquisition against a foreign enemy. Consequently when the great northern war broke out, Denmark joined the coalition against the Swedish king with little thought of the possible results to Norway. Finally, when victory failed to attend the young Swede and it was necessary for him to save the fragments, he turned upon Norway, determined to conquer it. The Danes had done nothing to fortify the Norwegian frontier; the national militia—such as had not been appropriated for the welfare of the Danish state proper—was ill clad and ill provided with ammunition and leaders. Nevertheless, the Norwegians proved themselves a match even for the valiant soldier king. The peasants rose, armed and equipped their own soldiers, provided money and food for their small forces, and fought so successfully that the Swedish leader who had won so many battles could not conquer even a small but important fortress on the coast. Finally Charles himself was shot by one of his own soldiers. The war ended thus abruptly enough. But Norway had at least proved her ability and her willingness to take care of herself in a most dangerous situation. Besides, she had played a conspicuous part in defeating the enemy at sea. Norwegian sailors had shown themselves the backbone of the Danish fleet and covered it with glory. Peter Wessel, better known as "Tordenskjold" (Thundershield), established his fame as a hero superior to them all. By his astounding boldness and bravery he time and again defeated the schemes of the Swedish king and at last forced him to return to Sweden without accomplishing anything. Such pluck and vigor, and the strong patriotic feeling manifested everywhere among the Norwegians, raised the Danish opinion considerably for the brethren on the other side of the sound. The name Norwegian became almost a name of honor. In verse and prose the "small nation among the mountains" was praised as an example of courage, faithfulness and bravery.

Still another and very different thing served to reestablish the Norwegians in public opinion. This was the contrast offered between the social-economical condition of the once free Danish peasantry and the conditions in Norway among the same class. A most shortsighted and lax policy on the part of the Danish government had allowed the big land owners gradually to deprive their free tenants of almost every vestige of personal liberty. Danish peasants had become almost serfs for the benefit of the landed gentry, who were thus supposed to secure cheap work and steady assistance. In Norway, on the other hand, the landed nobility did not have any such extended privileges. Every man lived on his own ground, possessed of little wealth but much freedom. Danish writers on economic subjects remarked upon this striking difference and found the topic fruitful of much declamation concerning the ancient freedom that dwelt among the Norwegian cliffs. The Norwegians themselves became declamatory and were accustomed to consider their country the cradle of freedom, the sacred soil on which no tyrant had ever set foot and from which Europe could draw afresh the old liberal spirit that had died out on the plains.

But the greatest spiritual achievement that Norway reached during these centuries of slow awakening was the giving to Danish-Norwegian literature of a man of such unique power as Ludvig Holberg. Hardly in the life of any nation has there been such a decisive change as occurred in the Danish-Norwegian intellectual life through the activity of this one man. Holberg's production in pure literature was in its main directions a perfectly novel undertaking, without model or support in previous Danish or Norwegian writings. His historical works, too, put other aims before the public and followed other paths than those hitherto customary in the two countries. (The sagas are, of course, not referred to here.) Besides, his philosophical thoughts moved in quite a different sphere from that which in his time was considered the realm of philosophy. And his comic-satyric writings were so unusual that they struck the public as wild and scandalous and unintelligible, even though amusing. When he first appeared, he stood as a representative of a wholly new taste, a wholly new view of life. The governing ideas or tastes that he found were his aversion. He brushed them all aside and undertook to reform that society for which he worked. And to an extent he really succeeded. He changed the people of those kingdoms as if they had been put into a new mould. He began as the lonely one, the stranger, giving and receiving only opposition. He ended with being the master before whom all bowed down. Whatever was thrown into oblivion by him was forgotten; the new introduced by him became the foundation on which Danish-Norwegian activities have built ever since. In reading his works we have even now the feeling of being at home. Back to him a tradition reaches which is fully alive. What existed before his day is dead and strange.

It has often been claimed that Holberg, in spite of his origin, was more Danish than Norwegian. The truth is that he was more European than either. His knowledge and his understanding of life were chiefly gained from his sojourn in other countries. He traveled more or less in Holland, France, Germany, Italy, and England. It is true that he lived the greater part of his life in Copenhagen, where he wrote his works and ended his days. But his character was formed and his genius trained before he settled there; and however Danish his audience and the immediate field of his activity, his temperament as a writer and his satirical vein remained Norwegian. There is something fresh,

[16]

bright and healthy about his writings, yet crisp and cold, that corresponds to the natural tendencies of mountaineers much more than to the population of a flat country.

In all these ways, then, came gradually that awakening of Norway which has filled the last few centuries and has finally in our own day brought the little country again into prominence as a producer of ideas. When nearly two hundred years ago the spirit of nationalism was once more really alive, its operations were not confined merely to sentiment or to literary achievement, but, as we should expect, affected also practical matters. The Norwegian people, in view of their strengthened economical condition, their considerable commerce, their means and will to defend themselves against foreign enemies, demanded from the Danish state increased consideration. They demanded that branch offices of the Danish government be established in their own foremost city; they demanded the foundation of a national bank and of a national university. For more than a hundred years these wishes were brought from time to time before the Danish king, the Norwegians declaring that they themselves would pay the expense for starting such new institutions. But they received in return only vague answers, subterfuges, or even plain refusal. The Danish government feared that if these demands were granted, Norway would speedily separate from the union. Denmark even thought Swedish machinations were to be detected in these requests, and chose the short-sighted policy of irritating curt refusal rather than arousing gratitude by compliance with such wishes.

And then at last came the events of the early nineteenth century. The Norwegian revolution that occurred in 1814 began shortly before with the coalition against Napoleon. During the Napoleonic wars the sympathies of Norway and Denmark had gone in opposite directions. Denmark, without taking part in the gigantic struggle, had been in favor of the French. The Norwegians were decidedly inclined toward England, with which they were in close commercial relations. It was, therefore, a severe shock to Norway and one that threw the country into famine, when Denmark declared war against England. It is true, the declaration was made only after outrageous insult by the English. But still it was a policy that brought every disadvantage and suffering on the Norwegians, who were without the least prospect of holding their own against a power that had command of the sea.

Previously, Napoleon had coveted an alliance with Denmark in order to use the Danish fleet to effect a landing on the English coast. To prevent this, the English in a time of apparently deep peace sent a fleet to Copenhagen and demanded the Danish men of war and Denmark's alliance. When these were refused, Copenhagen was bombarded and the fleet taken away. England's promise of alliance, however, was renewed. But the Danes, who thought chiefly of themselves, refused to consider the promise and sought refuge with

[18]

Napoleon. But now he had little interest in an alliance with Denmark since her fleet had been lost. It was Norway and Denmark that paid the price of that alliance, not Napoleon. Sweden meanwhile, under the leadership of Bernadotte, Napoleon's brother-in-law, had been persuaded to join the coalition against France. Then, after the war in 1813 and 1814, when the powers had succeeded in defeating Napoleon utterly, it was suggested that Denmark should pay the war indemnity; and that since Russia would not give up Finland, Denmark should cede Norway to Sweden as a recompense for Finland. Whatever the Norwegians had hitherto lacked to arouse their sense of honor this scandalous insult quickly supplied. The nation rose as one man, declared itself sovereign and the only power fit to decide upon its future action. In the teeth of Europe the Norwegians declared themselves a free and independent people, and gave themselves a constitution based upon the principles of the French revolution. This attitude somewhat surprised the combined powers, who expected no such manifestation of vigor on the part of the "small nation among the mountains."

Bernadotte, who was naturally the one most interested in the outcome, was commissioned to lead his army against the rebellious Norwegians and compel them to obedience under the will of combined Europe. There is no doubt that Bernadotte, with his well-trained and well-equipped army against an insufficient body of national militia, however brave, could in the long run have accomplished that for which he was sent,

But he decided to use more humane and politically more safe means. He was eager to end the war and have the glory of coming to terms with the Norwegians without further bloodshed. A party existed in Norway favoring a union with Sweden. Sweden seemed to be the more natural ally, and some political reasons at the time also pointed in the same direction. The idea was not at all unfavorably regarded by the younger more progressive patriots. Bernadotte, as the plenipotentiary of the Swedish nation, agreed to accept the Norwegian constitution as the future supreme law of the country and preserve the rights and privileges as guaranteed by this law. Norway on its side agreed by its representatives to join Sweden in a union under a common king and to give certain precedence to Sweden as the larger country. This policy, so wisely started by Bernadotte, or King Carl Johan, as he later became, was never altogether comprehended by Sweden. The Swedes attempted to make the union more and more real, such as that, for example, between Scotland and England.

The Norwegians, however, having the disastrous experience with Denmark to look back upon, steadily refused to become a "province" for a second time. In fact, the inclination was to consider the union a rather unfair bargain, granting greater rights to Sweden than to Norway; although it was well understood that Norway should be represented in the union as an entirely free and independent nation and receive due regard as such. The squabbles raised on minor matters gradually grew to bigger and bigger dimensions until in 1905 a rupture became imminent.

Ever since 1892, when the Storting first decided that Norway should have her own Minister of Foreign Affairs and her separate consuls, there had been a bitter strife between Norway and Sweden. The break came during the Michelson-Lövland ministry, when it was unanimously passed that Norway should have its own consulates. King Oscar refused to sanction the measure. The ministry then resigned, and it was impossible for the king to form a new one. On June seventh, 1905, the declaration was made that Oscar had ceased to rule Norway. Thus the ninety-year-old union with Sweden came to an end. Two days later the pure Norwegian flag (deprived of the union mark) was hoisted upon the fortresses and warships. On August thirteenth a general vote was cast by the people of the realm which almost unanimously sanctioned the act of supreme power. In September the Karlstad negotiations took place.

Horrors brought about by unpardonable levity and political short-sightedness might at this time have precipitated a war and needless bloodshed. But an amicable agreement was reached, largely through the efforts of the just and prudent statesman, Christian Michelson, who, by his tactful, yet resolute actions, proved himself in that difficult time a greater leader and a better patriot than many an over-zealous contemporary.

In November the Norwegian people were again asked to vote as to whether they would choose a monarchical form of government or a republican. With an overwhelming majority they chose to maintain the kingdom. Norway's ancient throne thus rose again to its former prerogative. The Storting elected as king the Danish prince Carl, giving him the title of Haakon the Seventh. On November twenty-fifth the new king, together with Queen Maud and the crown prince Olav, made a royal entry into the metropolis, welcomed by cheering throngs. The new state was immediately recognized by the powers, and the whole world, filled with admiration, rejoiced with the "small nation among the mountains" because it had ended its long struggle for independence happily and in peace.

LONG generation ago when Ibsen and Grieg and their contemporaries were entering ripe manhood, Norway was scarcely the modernized country that she has since become. These men's impressions, moreover, of their native land were largely drawn from a period still further away. Their works are reminiscent of the time of their youth, often colored, too, by the light of imagination which ever tends to fall from the present back upon the past. In that earlier Norway all material conditions were more primitive than now, even more crude and hard; though not less interesting as manifestations of human experience. Differences in temper and modes of living produced by climate and natural surroundings were sharper and of deeper dye. The great length from North to South of the Scandinavian peninsula—greater even than that of the Atlantic seaboard of the United States—caused and will probably always cause marked divergence in the types of people and habits of life at the extremities of the country. But not merely so. A difference also strongly marked existed then between the West and the East in Norway itself, without regard to the rest of the peninsula. Under the touch of modern facilities and conveniences this difference is melting away. In the middle of the last century, however, it was still visible, not only in the physical nature of the country

[23]

—which of course has not changed—but in the language, in the life of the people, their character and manners, even in their feelings. So great was this divergence between the West and the East of Norway that some historians have thought the people to be of different origin. Such was not the case, but nature had indeed shaped them in different moulds.

The first views of the western coast of Norway, when sailing in toward it from the sea, make one almost crouch under overwhelming discomfort and oppression. Far out in the open sea one is met by rows of low, gray rocks, like guardsmen that look with ominous eye on every passing ship. Around these the waves break in continuous restless fall, while above gulls and seabirds rise and dip with chilling screams. Some uncanny friendship seems to quiver between that sea, those rocks, and the shrieking birds. This vanguard passed, one big black range of mountains appears, rising from the coast and defying the surging sea. No trace visible of human existence in this desert of sea and stone, nor does one expect or wish for any. But suddenly, as if by magic, some small seaport shows itself on the naked coast—just a glimpse of white houses between the cliffs, boatsheds and skiffs on the shore, ships at anchor —then the whole is hidden behind the next point, and there remain only scattered creeping herds of sheep. Soon again nothing but the wind and the bare rocks.

Our vessel now steers into one of the many fjords that penetrate the mass of stone. Rocks and shelves close in upon us and the sea disappears. A door has suddenly shut between us and the world outside. The life wherein our thoughts and desires had before been concentrated seems to sink flutteringly out of sight forever. With a gasp we look toward what is coming, and see the New rising in threatening majesty. We breathe an air that seems to bring death to all who cannot gain new lungs, in body and in mind. For a time all before and behind is closed. But again a sudden door opens ahead upon unexpected vistas. The mountains draw aside, and green shores, white churches, and cozy dwellings smile brightly and familiarly. Big swaying birches with long branches hang over the water, silvery brooks jump playfully from the side of the mountain straight out into the air, break into foam and disappear like a dream. From the sea to the coal-black forest around the upper row of meadows, all is gay and light. But we have time for only one single free breath, for now again the whole tract of vision is filled with gray hunch-backed mountains. Those nearest press upon us almost to suffocation. Above and behind them rises another set, naked from foot to summit, broken into a thousand peaks and grooves, jags and rents—blinding white snow lying in sharp edges, drifts, and blotches on the blue background. On and on through the fjord we go, turning into its arms and outlets, winding around its points and peninsulas, and everywhere are the snowy peaks. They rule the whole horizon and question the traveler who ventures to intrude upon their domain.

Between these dizzy peaks that storm the very heavens, between the narrow green slopes on the mountainside, where tiny homesteads cling to the stone for very life and seem to need but a breath to push them into the sea, we reach at last a valley. Now everything broadens; here are plains, more houses, more woods—resting places for the eye and the heart. But again we move by. Cold glimpses of snow shine from afar, a raging river bursts forth from the opening of the valley, breathes out an icy breath, and winds in the wildest twists and turns till it falls here or there into a deep lair, where it remains like a wild beast devouring prey caught in a mad race. The goer on foot beside that river finds wet grass standing in small clusters along the road, raw cliffs hanging above, and a brown mountain lake waiting below for his unwary footsteps. And behind him every hill seems to rise like a live thing, low bushes creep up and up, bent and crooked, array themselves against the horizon, step into line and say: "In you may come, but out——?" And suddenly he is aware that in the river, in the hills, in the lakes, in the winds, live those evil powers, the giants and the trolls, against whom the old gods fought in vain. And there, beyond, are the last heights where no human dwelling subsists, where the mountains rule undisturbed and hurtle down their avalanches on the small ant-like things called men.

What is to be understood about the land where such a nature dominates? Surely that the modes of living in the East either did not exist in the West or existed under such changed conditions as to influence the people quite differently. Though once large woods covered the coast, the West in recent times has had little lumber business or cultivation of forests, and men's livelihood has been chiefly gained from the fisheries. A few trees, indeed, climb the mountainsides where the rocks shelter them from the salt winds; but on the whole the vegetation is confined to grass (the chief sustenance of the sheep that are left out winter and summer), and the brown heather that lies and trembles in the wind. In the valleys, it is true, there are woods; and woods most wonderfully conformed to the nature around them. The predominant tree in the valleys is the strong, powerful fir, which presses its deep-going root into the fissures of the rocks—not a tree that dreams, like the spruce of the East, but one that lifts its broad, bushy crown far up in the wind, fights the storm, and keeps itself in courage by chanting, like the old warriors, hard alliterating rhymes of battle. High and airy it is for a man under these fir branches, fresh and bright among their yellow trunks, and he grows strong from dwelling beneath their coarse needles and healthy from the resinous air. The dainty white-stemmed birch, growing alike in valley and on mountain, is the lightsome sister of the sturdy fir. Hardiest of trees, it yet gives as nothing else does a tender delicacy and comeliness to that stern nature. On the barest mountain it sways, in the foam of the surf it dyes its foliage, and the very home of the glacier it bravely storms. Close to the sea, indeed, or to the eternal ice,

[27]

the birch loses its long curls and its delicate upright bearing; but it maintains to the last its feminine grace. Even in the most barren places it gives pleasure to the eye, and in spring it brings to its desolate surroundings a most exquisite fragrant greeting of summer. Often it is the one object in those severe landscapes which can melt the heart to softness by its beauty or lift to faith by its bright, successful courage.

A sensitive mind cannot but be deeply impressed by the effect that this iron nature has had upon the people who lived in it. In countries where natural conditions are varied and bountiful, the people may be independent and open to many different avenues of influence. But when nature has a strong individuality and offers few ways of gaining a living, it is likely to become tyrannical and stamp both the inner and the outer man. In such a country conditions often produce fierce struggle, and every human being who will not or cannot assimilate himself to these conditions is dwarfed or dies. It is easy to understand that people who sit in the cold shadow of high mountains, who day after day look at black rock and blue glaciers, who are snowed down for a month and a half at a time and live in constant fear lest the avalanche carry their homes into the depths below, people whose hope for a livelihood is in the dark winter weather and on a sea full of danger, and who at any time must be prepared to venture life itself to gain that scanty living— it is easy to understand how such people bear the effect of their life in their character. Unless some ameliorating influence comes in counteraction, man feels strangely deserted and feeble in such a nature. But this feeling of feebleness has a very different effect upon different persons. Some give up the struggle at once; hopelessly bent under the weight, they sink slowly down into a dark abyss of melancholy and pass the rest of their life as if in fear and in prison. Others are petrified under the icy conviction that daily life is governed by an inflexible fate against which it is useless to struggle. Such men and women are often strong but hard, having divested themselves of all idea of happier prospects for the future. Though they go into danger calm and cool, they pass with silent indifference all that might coax the heart to open itself to mildness. Endurance, courage, and expediency they possess in plenty, but everything is as if frozen by the awful conviction that beyond your fate you will never get. Others whose imagination is too strong to be extinguished are filled with vague images of horrors and see no advance for themselves except by bending down before the mysterious powers of nature. They seek to ally themselves with these powers, to pry into their will and please them, and perhaps even solicit their assistance. By such minds nature is transformed into the living beings of superstitious fear who have man at their mercy.

Thus all are likely to be cowed by such a fierce nature; bowing down before it, some in melancholy, others in obduracy, still others in superstition. True liberation of mind is seldom acquired. And though such nature also has a power of creating Christian

resignation, yet even that God-fearing spirit is often
as hard and sinister as the physical surroundings.
Fanaticism finds there peculiarly favorable conditions
and burns like fire in dry grass. The general imagination easily absorbs the idea of God's wrath and eternal
punishment, but has little room for tenderness and a
reconciling love. He who wishes to see this ice and
stone nature of western Norway embodied in one great
picture must read Ibsen's *Brand*, the most tremendous and most one-sided expression of this nature that
our literature possesses.

The whole West was long bound, too, by traditions
and had a decidedly old-fashioned character. The
houses were many and small, low and dark. Little was
seen of modern improvement. The agricultural imple-
ments were more fit for a museum than for a farmer;
and the conveyances—the cart, the carjol, or the sled
in winter—were the terror of more than one traveler.
Within the house the "high seat" at the end of the
long table was still reserved for the head of the family.
Everything seemed centuries old. In language, in
dress, and in social intercourse the old dignity and
ceremonial still prevailed. The bride still rode to
church with a shining silver crown on her long, spread-
out hair and with silver brooches on her white linen.
The old strange songs and marches were played before
her procession and her wedding feast was not given in
bright, open rooms as in the East, but in the small,
close dwellings where the old timber was black as ebony
from the smoke and soot of generations. These darker

sides of western life would at once seize the eye and
the heart of any observer, and have certainly exercised a
most powerful influence upon the national character.

But western nature has a sunny, lucid side, too, and
has given to the popular mind a corresponding uplift.
The brightness of nature particularly breaks forth
in Spring. For those crags and valleys have a Spring
whose sweetness is nowhere found in the East. If the
sun has been missing during the long winter, its reap-
pearance is so much the more wonderfully prophetic of
new life, new joy, and fresh power. Winter does not
disappear by inches, as in the East, and Spring does
not come with a mingling of snow and water. One
leaps away and the other comes with a bound. Yesterday was bleak Winter. Today spirits of Summer live
already in air, soil, and water. They dance on the melt-
ing ice of the streams, they sail in with the soft breeze
from the sea, they smile from the bright sky, and they
exhale from every bare spot; for the grass grows up
to the very edge of the snow. From these Spring and
Summer-day visions of a sea as smooth as glass or rock-
ing between sunny mountains, from green and fragrant
fields that break into flower while yet in the very arms
of ice, from a salt breeze bringing news of foreign
shores—from these arise the light and beauty that
play with such exquisite freshness and warmth over
the darker features of that rock-girt land. Herein is
the source of the blue depth and giddy vivacity of
imagination which has characterized the people of the
West—the dancing waves of playful humor, the

flashes of wit that seem like living sunbeams in the shut-up valley of pensive thought. From such visions as these came the wonderful softness of Ole Bull's strings which sang the secret of that Spring to the whole world. From these was caught the musical lilt in the speech of the West and likewise the peculiar delicate beauty of many homes—homes that were crowned with this beauty in spite of their inaccessibility and of any suspiciousness they may have had of the world outside. Where these ameliorating influences from without have been allowed to become a power, where the deep, earnest simplicity of soul and the unshaken determination which this nature produces have received their measure of light and heat, there one meets such warmth of temperament, such truthfulness in speech and manner, such purity and beauty of thought, that no nature seems capable of a more exalting influence upon a nation's life. If the blue sky and its stars have thus been able to look down into the depths of man, the thwarting power has been counteracted and education has been gained without a stunting of growth. Many of our noblest men and women have exemplified this happy fusion. They have won breadth without losing depth, have matured into tenderness and beauty and yet not lost in primitiveness and solidity. They are the finest product of our land. Neither the West nor the East may wholly claim them, for they belong to the world, contributing through their own rounded development the best our nation has to offer to the general consciousness of humanity.

*   *   *   *   *   *   *   *

When one has stayed at the coast for some time, it is impossible on crossing the mountains into the East not to be astonished at the sudden breadth of the horizon. Although the Westerner during a long sojourn in the East always feels a lack and longs for his accustomed scenery, yet it is a great gain to have before him for some time these large cultivated districts and to feel a loosening of the tension caused by the threatening force of the mountains. Here in Eastland are broad, expansive valleys that end in broad rivers. Here shining streams glide down through meadows full of thick luxuriant grass and past fields of tall grain, or the tract slopes gently down toward a lake with low shores and jutting points that look like fields and woods swimming on the water. The houses are either placed on the top of the slope where they gaze out and greet each other with bright windows, or else they are along the roads in the bottom of a valley near a lake, while all the fat meadows, yellow grainfields, and dark, spruce-clad hills are behind them. They lie there sunning themselves in broad, safe comfort, in quiet, everyday happiness, roomy and cozy, with gardens in front and big trees in the yard. Seen at a distance, they all seem to be at their noonday rest and to have plenty of leisure to look out over the water and the road. There is something self-complacent and sure about them, yet one has a feeling of their being always ready to open their large rooms in unlimited hospitality. Means of an easier existence in this region are evident even in the soil, which is nowhere so stony as in the West but seems to invite road-making and railroad-building. Fields and meadows and the big forests also speak of more abundance. People here have open, bright faces such as are seldom seen in the West. Everything in property and income is on a larger scale; one feels almost well-to-do oneself and finds life lenient and agreeable.

It has been said, however, and with some truth, that the spiritual power of the West is greater, and that most of our best men have come from the coast and the mountains. Agriculture gives steadiness and persistence to conditions because its results can be gained by regular work and do not depend on chance and luck. But on the other hand, it does not give that elasticity of spirit, that flight of thought, that venturesome courage and perseverance of will, which are fostered by the life on the shore. The clay soil which clings to the foot also weighs down the soul, the uniform, everyday life makes the imagination gray and creeping, the will slack, and the whole mental life shallow and dry. Even in the far days of old it was thus. Even then the better portion of national strength was in the West. By people from the West, Iceland was populated and continents discovered, and there was the true home of the Vikings. Thence alone could be drawn their courage, able to battle with the unknown, their deep earnestness, their imaginative freshness, their salty humor.

But these opinions regarding the two portions of the country are not tenable in every particular. The basis of them is too narrow. For the eastern imagination is dark-eyed and dreamy though slow in action. Though it lacks the transparent blue, the rapid swing, that characterize the spirit of the West, yet it possesses its own mighty enchantment. If the West has the sea and the mountains, the East has no less potent an influence—the stately forest. The tree which gives individuality to that forest is the spruce—a kind not found in the West, but in the East having a growth and color not manifested anywhere else in Europe. When one faces these armies of black trees with their tall, spire-like tops and low, swaying branches that seem to cover up some hidden treasure, one stands before the Romance of the East. Here in the unbroken quiet of majesty where only a falling twig, a frightened animal, or a band of lurking gipsies interrupt the solitude— here the dark-eyed huldre lives. Here the arrow of the huntsman strikes unawares old churchbells that have been silent for a hundred years. Here the air is heavy with tales of the past which the stiff-bearded forest giants tell each other over and again—tales of the life they once saw, the chivalrous plays and festivals on the noble estates that are no more. For they also saw the great places deserted during the Black Death, and as the years slipped by, the giants quietly moved on into the yard, gazed through the windows into the empty rooms, and have held guard for centuries around the abandoned homes. If in the moonlight one walks along the edge of these forests and looks at the moving black spires against the sky, feels the cool air they

breathe forth and inhales the fresh odor of their needles, listening as they whisper together in indescribable
moaning singsong, never forgotten when once heard,
one understands that they have indeed a secret to watch
over.   They are the source of the countless songs and
stories, the unknown kingdom where the creative imagination finds a home.   One understands that if ever these
woods were laid quite low, something great and important would be lost to the nation; all would be turned
into the barren ground of cold materiality and the
soul would be panting for the woods of old with their
shade, their dew, their fragrance.

Perhaps these emanations of mystery and greatness
whispered to the listening mind are not wholly lost even
when the forest goes forth on its practical mission of
service to the economic well-being of its country, when
the yellow logs have left their quiet home on the hills
and have sung their last hymn in the sawmill or said
goodbye to the fatherland and sailed across the ocean.
As the old trusty giants sink one after another under
the axe, the groans and crash of the breaking down
resound in the forest, and their comrades whisper the
sad news far off in the distant woods.   In the evening
the workmen gather in the huts, the fire glows lustily,
coffee is cooked, and burning torches light up the
fantastic scene.   And then the falling giants exhale
their first lore—the romance of their stories; while out
in the shed the horses shiver in the cold.

Soon the forest has ended the first part of its journey, and the lumber is turned into the broad way of

general usefulness. One portion remains in the country
built into bridges and houses, and looks at its brethren
that still stand and murmur in the wind. Its life in
freedom is over, the age of its possibly higher purpose
begun. Yet faint traces of its former existence remain.
From now on it tells ghost stories, in dark outhouses
or far in the country when it has become very old.
Other portions go perhaps to greater events but to the
same whispering silence. The magnificent trees which
become ships and carry their comrades away with them,
may lie, even in the great centres of trade, and talk
in the depth of the sea or breathe up from it those
strange stories which the sailors bring home with them.
. . . . . Our forest thus enters the life of the
great world. But the poets and dreamers at home
never quite cease to miss it and mourn over it. They
touch more gently the standing trees because of their
comrades that are gone, and to their listening hearts
the forest mysteries are open secrets.

HENRIK WERGELAND[1]

N 1814 occurred the greatest single event in the history of Norway during the nineteenth century. It was the meeting at Eidsvold of a little body of statesmen to frame a national constitution for Norway. The union with Denmark having been broken by the treaty of Kiel, Norway was determined to decide its destiny for itself. To this Norwegian Congress was sent a young preacher and teacher from Christiansand named Nicolai Wergeland.[2] He had been previously known in national affairs, as is witnessed by his stirring appeal for a national university; which indeed had been founded in 1811. He soon became one of the most prominent and influential members of the Congress. He was aggressively antagonistic toward Denmark, whose treatment of Norway he called criminal. The idea of a voluntary union with Sweden, which sprang up in the Assembly, had at first his sympathy and soon his earnest defense. He formed a warm attachment to the new Swedish king, Carl Johan, Napoleon's former leader, Maréchal Bernadotte, whose brilliant exploits as a soldier and whose generous benefactions in the North had won for him many other patriots as staunch as Wergeland. The king on his side admired Wergeland's shrewd caution, practical ability, and patriotic breadth of view; and he was will-

[1]Pronounced Vairg' (e)lan; g hard, e short, slightly sounded.
[2]See Frontispiece.

[38]

Henrik Wergeland

ing to recognize and reward them, especially since in part through Wergeland's efforts a union of Norway with Sweden was finally effected.

To this position of political importance, intellectual leadership, and friendly relation with the ruling powers, Henrik Wergeland was heir. Though of a character and temper quite different from his father and having an entirely different career, he too became a political and intellectual leader. At the time of the Eidsvold Congress Henrik was a child of six. Not long afterward Nicolai Wergeland received the living at Eidsvold parish and for the rest of his life remained there as Dean in the State Church (Lutheran) and as occasional court preacher. At Eidsvold Henrik passed his boyhood.

While a child he was not considered remarkable, but a little later his genius developed as suddenly as a northern spring. In 1825 he became a student at the new national university. Two years afterward he was already known as a poet of indisputable originality, turbid and turgid, but with extraordinary luxuriance and primitiveness. Poem after poem appeared, lyrics and romances, farces, dramas and tragedies; and all the while he was studying for his final degree in divinity and was writing steadily for newspapers. A tremendous poem, seven hundred and twenty pages long, a kind of philosophic epic called *Creation, Man, and Messias,* he tossed off almost extempore. It is a remarkable proof of his easy productivity at this time. He was a hot-headed youth, boiling over with plans and

[39]

ideas, a republican and a revolutionist, an ultra-
Norwegian, a friend of the people, an advocate of the
low and down-trodden; always maturing new schemes
for popular elevation and improvement, never thinking
of his own profit, continually exposing himself to new
rebuffs, yet never disheartened, always fresh and vigorous, full of enthusiasm and optimistic faith. In all
these ways he was said to be like his grandfather, a
"turbulent head," whose family belonged in Bergens
Stift on the West coast, a region where people are
known as among the liveliest, brightest, most hot-
blooded and enterprising in the whole country.

The Congress of 1814 had brought to Norway independence as a nation. But the liberty granted by the
new constitution had now to be made real and practical
by growth in the inner mental life of the people itself.
For though a people receive liberty as a gift or at small
cost, it will no less surely have to earn all and pay
gradually what it did not pay at first. The national
instinct now demanded manifestations in literature,
language, art, science, and in enlightened public
opinion, which should justify the nation's claims to
recognition from other nations. The break from the
domination of Denmark and the tie with Sweden both
called out an exaggerated defensiveness and emphasis
of self in the Norwegians. They needed a leader who
would incorporate their new aims and their new consciousness of power and will—a leader whose activity
would be the best justification of their claims, and who
would unite their scattered forces under one head. He

who best represented these aspirations and answered these needs was the young poet, barely out of his teens, but already brimming over with the sense of his mission and eager to fulfill the patriotic obligations with which he had charged himself.

Like poet-politicians of the time in other countries, Wergeland welcomed the July revolution of 1830 in France as the coming of a golden age, and watched European politics with the greatest eagerness. He thought a republic the best form of government, but he made few if any efforts to force that form upon his own country. He advocated the idea rather as the last logical conclusion of his political philosophy than as a practical solution of immediate difficulties. The notion of general brotherhood also appealed to him, and this led him to advocate a Scandinavian union or federation of states, for which the United States and its constitution gave him inspiration. But even while he was dreaming of a Northern union, his attention was necessarily drawn to the direct interests of Norway itself.

A smouldering conflict had long existed between the two layers of population in Norway—the native Norwegian on the one side and on the other the official class. This class had sprung partly from generations of Danes sent to Norway as executives, and partly from other foreigners who mingled rather with the Danish element than with the native peasantry. The conflict between these two elements was now bearing its first fruit in the formation of an ultra-Norwegian party.

As soon as that happened, the cosmopolitan Wergeland became more Norwegian than anybody; and the opposition to the encroachment of either of the other northern states found its most determined spokesman in him who had just before been advocating a Scandinavian union. Yet there was no real contradiction in this. His ideal was in essence national, and the union he thought of was to be merely a combination of kindred nationalities. His attitude was largely misunderstood, however, owing to the bitterness with which he was attacked. Yet his behavior during this long political strife savored more of political wisdom than that of his adversaries. For he represented a sound, necessary instinct of self-preservation, a keen, clear-sighted effort to protect the national from outside usurpation till it had grown strong enough to maintain itself without defensive measures. Half a generation had passed since the adoption of the constitution, and still all forms of life were as yet running in the old grooves. But now a peculiar restlessness became evident in the nation at large, a feeling that the constitution so adored was a pledge which the nation had to fulfill. Of the significance of this restlessness Henrik Wergeland seems to have been more clearly aware than anyone; and he did more to keep the inner stirring alive and urge it on to manifestation in deeds. His poetry at this time possesses the same restlessness and stormy character as the popular feeling expressed. It sprang from a sense of new power, not quite conscious of itself or certain of its aim. That he was right later events have fully proved. The background of his conception of nationality was not dreamy sentiment. Though poetical, it was not mystical, but was the thought of natural progress and was an ideally rational aim such as both nations and individuals must hold.

To understand the conflict in the nation at this time, it must be remembered that the Norwegian peasants were not and had never been serfs immovably attached to the land, as had been the case in other countries. They were not in subjection to territorial lords, but were themselves landowners, rulers of small private domains. In the middle ages they had been a most proud, independent and self-governing class of people. Only gradually had their share in government slipped away from them (cf. pp 5-7), and they still retained their dignity and independence of feeling. To be a peasant in Norway was to belong to the truly national element of the population, to be among those who owned their homes, cultivated their lands, and kept their profits. The opposition to existing conditions which now arose and created the ultra-Norwegian party was active chiefly in this independent, land-owning peasantry.

The opposition was indeed both political and literary, but in its political aspect it was an effort of the peasant class against the official class, who were mostly Danish in sympathy and who as the peasants felt had dominated politics too long. Members of the official class had indeed been in the majority in the Congress of 1814, but the democratic ideal then prevalent everywhere had so operated in them, too, that they had

[43]

themselves abolished nobility and the idea of an upper house of government. They fixed the right to vote merely upon ownership of land and official position. By these two standards the greater share in government would in time come to the peasants, since there would always be more landowners than officials. At first the peasants, in their feeling of political immaturity united their votes for the official class; and the early national assemblies after 1814 had been mainly composed of members of this class. To their praise it must be said that they showed themselves worthy of their traditions. They maintained the dignity of the assembly and the rights of the constitution against the repeated attempts made by Sweden to increase Swedish privileges in the union and to press Norway down to an inferior rank. The peasant members joined bravely in this fight to preserve the constitution intact. Gradually the population woke to the fact that the ruling power belonged to the people at large instead of to a class. Then the unfortunate heady attempt began to push the officials out of power—an attempt which in time proved almost distressingly successful. Much ill-feeling was aroused. The officials, who still counted among their number by far the most intelligent, best-trained people, saw with horror the power gradually lodge in the hands of the more numerous but less prepared peasantry.

Although Henrik Wergeland was the son of a state official (church and state being one), he sympathized most heartily with the peasantry. He immediately joined their ranks and became their spokesman against the "tyranny" of the officials. He undoubtedly saw that the peasants were not yet ready for their political mission, but he also knew that they could not acquire political maturity without exercising their faculties; and since they insisted on grasping what the constitution gave them, he wished to help them in their school of political experience.

Naturally in the literary part of the opposition Wergeland was also active. In fact, he was the chief figure. The whole strife, indeed, was a strife between two opposed cultures. The one represented by Wergeland had mainly English and French presuppositions, leaned upon the eighteenth century and its political continuation in the July revolution, and upon English poetical literature and philosophy and rationalistic humanism. On the other side was the German-Danish culture, which leaned upon the reaction by the German romanticists against the eighteenth century. Religiously, it clung to the old orthodoxy as a reaction against rationalism; and politically, it was the first expression, on Norwegian ground, of the general European conservative relapse, after the striving in 1830 for liberty and revolutionary idealism.

In this literary side of the conflict, the pro-Danish party, however active many of its members had been in securing independence in government, could not see much prospect for intellectual life in Norway if it was separated from the Danish. At the time the pro-Danish view seemed right. Danish literature was in its golden age when a whole Parnassus of writers made Copenhagen the special home of muses and graces. The intellectual party in Norway looked to Denmark as its true home and as having the atmosphere for true literary production. The contrast between the youthful efforts of clumsy Norwegian imitators and the finished works of the polished Danes seemed too great to allow hope of a literary life at all equal to the Danish. The reasons then apparent lay in the immaturity of almost everything in Norway—the narrow, provincial character of the social world, the political disturbances, the patriotic bombast, the crudeness of the general national life with its "ignorant peasantry" as chief element, the lack of a capital city that could really lead, and the absence of an aristocracy that might establish a standard of taste and give a refined tone to society.

These opinions of the pro-Danish Norwegians were confirmed in Denmark itself. The Danes, with their whole tradition from Holberg down, felt superior to the Norwegians. What writers had Norway had previous to the separation who were not influenced by Danish life? And what had it since? The fact that Norwegians had for many generations been compelled to go abroad for their highest education explains in part the absence of a distinctly Norse literature. And at the present moment they had no writer to boast of as their very own except Henrik Wergeland, no one who could claim the broad field and hold the attention of the public as he did. But of him the anti-national party had no high opinion. In Denmark all Norwegian writers were ignored, and Wergeland's works were scarcely known till late in the century. The pro-Danish among his countrymen were alienated by his stormy lyric, his visions of heaven and earth, and his disregard for forms and laws held sacred by the critics. The novelty of his mere appearance stunned them, and the voluminous often confused nature of his productivity, letting good and bad, perfect and imperfect, go to press and reach the public red hot, made them bitter and scornful toward this new power that claimed to be so thoroughly national. They turned away from the tumult at home to the other land, where such storm and stress did not exist and whence they could receive a superior culture and æsthetic pleasure.

Their spokesman was a young student of the same age as Henrik Wergeland by the name of Welhaven. Welhaven's pronounced interest in æsthetics, his conception of poetry as expressing calmness and clearness only, his dislike of any political excess, and his shy, sensitive, melancholy temperament, all made him the born contrast and sworn opponent of Wergeland. And in Welhaven Wergeland found his most merciless critic, one who seemed often to take pleasure in seeing nothing but chaos and leaving him bare of any poetical qualities whatever. According to Welhaven, other ideals than Wergeland's must be presented to the nation. These ideals he himself showed in a cycle of sonnets called *The Dawn of Norway*. In these he declared it would be folly to denounce Danish culture when there was nothing to put in its place; and he pointed to the inner rejuvenation which alone can lead to true liberty. Above all he condemned Wergeland because in his superciliousness he would deliver the nation over to intellectual suicide by prohibiting foreign influences even though such poverty existed at home.

But Wergeland did not wish to oppose Danish culture to a suicidal degree. He did not wish to reduce the Norwegians to a barbarous condition. What he saw and insisted upon was that only through self-activity could the native and the national grow strong enough to maintain itself in later contact with foreign cultures. The conflict, of course, need not have existed at all if the native Norwegian element had felt able to assimilate without loss of individuality. But there was the danger.

Consciously or unconsciously Welhaven then and ever afterward misrepresented the attitude of Wergeland. To Welhaven the highest culture seemed concentrated in Danish life. To Wergeland culture was universal, and it was this universal culture which he wished his country made fit to receive by concentration and development within itself. The process of preparation was in a measure advocated by both men, but in different ways. The struggle between the pro-Danish and the ultra-Norwegians lasted throughout Wergeland's life. Although Welhaven soon withdrew personally, his theories were maintained by a body of close friends.

As might have been foreseen, succeeding events have proved that both leaders were to an extent right. But for the moment Wergeland's was the agency most necessary for the growth of the nation. And one thing is certain—he was never so bigoted as his adversaries. His enthusiasm for a national literature was indeed exaggerated and tumultuous, but it was necessary and found its response in national pride and national ambition. The later preëminence of Norwegian literature has fully justified his zeal. His adversaries, however, would not grant its value and significance even for the time. To them it seemed evident that Norway could not change her condition. Even the language they thought too barbarous for poetical expression and far inferior in melody to the Danish. This also Wergeland combated, and pointed out the superior right of Norwegian words, both because they were Norwegian and sounded true and familiar to people of Norway, and because they had a more suggestive fullness of volume and thus approached the strong resonant tone of the old original language.

In the heat of battle the pro-Danish often forgot that they had to do with their own countrymen, and their superior culture did not prevent them from calling their opponents barbarians and spoilers. Wild combats took place in the newspapers, and, at times of special excitement, in the streets as well. Wergeland was of course the arch enemy whose aspirations, political and poetical, were unworthy of polite consideration.

A glance at the literary activity of Wergeland from 1830 to 1840 shows that he understood better than anybody the historical justification of the political turmoil because he saw the ideal meaning hidden under the noisy quarrel. Himself pushing along and exciting the popular feeling and being in turn excited by it, he was in the happiest sympathy with his people; that kind of sympathy which is the surest footing for any poet, however vague and obscure the sympathy may be on the part of the nation at large. His poems, from the epos of humanity down to songs for the seventeenth of May (the day of independence), mirror the thoughts and feelings of the time. His farces, too, were political and polemical. And besides being incessantly active as a poet, he was an indefatigable journalist. His newspaper articles were innumerable, mostly anonymous, but in a style easily recognized. Scarcely a subject that roused the interest of the day escaped his active pen. Destined only for the moment, scratched down on sudden impulses, most of the articles cannot be properly judged if torn from their connection. They are chiefly an expression of that constant watchfulness with which he threw a hint here and a hint there, thus giving what the infant democracy needed—direction and guidance. They helped to keep the people in a constant vibration, conscious of how much was yet to be done, how many demands had yet to be satisfied. The articles were in style epigrammatic, often careless; but they contained so much positive and practical information, they had so much power to agitate and to illumine subjects of general importance that at the time they were of great value.

Wergeland's participation in the events of the day, both political and literary, was so prominent that in the eyes of the pro-Danish he was the incarnation of the ultra-Norwegian party in its wildest, most disagreeable form. To Welhaven and his party Wergeland was not only impossible as a poet, but equally impossible as a politician. In fact, he was no politician, merely a political demagogue of the worst type; following both in literature and government arbitrary individualistic principles, advocating isolation and therefore suicide. If, as a matter of fact, we know nothing of Wergeland but his restless activity in the political agitation, he may indeed appear to have been a mere revolutionary party leader, nothing more than the chief of a radical faction. But there are other sides of his busy life that reveal quite a different character. In spite of all his restlessness, he pursued calmly and logically his purpose of raising the nation as a whole to the level of its true patriotic aspirations. The chief object in his life as a citizen was to increase the fund of education and culture in the nation at large. Education for all he regarded as the broad basis of a true democracy. Herein lies the substantial difference between his conception of national culture and that of the pro-Danish. The pro-Danish saw in "culture" the flower of historical development confined to a select few, to those who possessed intellectual maturity, superior knowledge and elevated views of life. Such culture would necessarily be æsthetic in character. Though it claimed to be national, it was in fact mainly aristocratic. It

81710

stood aloof, studied and observed "the people" as an interesting phenomenon, and treated in like manner the myths and tales wherein the obscure past, the primitive stage of the people's life, still partly revealed itself. The result of such observation would naturally be artistic reproduction in song and tale; thus justifying, for art, the attitude taken toward these phenomena.

But in Wergeland's conception of the national life this view of the people had no part. To him the myths and tales that interested the æsthetes were superstitions, reminiscences of the time when the people were not as yet awake. The "child of nature" must be changed into a conscious being, master of his conditions, a free citizen, aware of his rights and duties. The romantic conception doted upon the *dreams* of the national spirit, but Wergeland demanded the higher consciousness which produces beings who can think. To Wergeland culture was for all. It was a development of intellect, knowledge, reason, morality, sense of duty. Welhaven's conception was far more æsthetic and artistic. The one poet was a philanthropist and a practical philosopher; the other was an artist and an æsthetic philosopher.

"Our time," said Wergeland, "has understood that the basis of the happiness and life of a nation is general culture. If it is not general, the efforts of a few individuals to raise the national level can be but uncertain." Such declarations as these show him most directly and clearly as in the broadest sense a man of the people. They prove his right to receive the love which

Henrik Wergeland Statue, Fargo, North Dakota. Part of the inscription is:

Lyric Poet, Father of Norwegian Literature,
Friend of the Poor and Oppressed,
Champion of the Weak against the Strong,
Opened the Doors of Norway to the Jews.

The Statue is a donation from Norway to the United States.

the people bore him even early in his career. Political preparation or education were not needed by anybody to understand his warm sympathy which bloomed in a thousand acts of charity. Nobody loved the common people as he did, nobody sought so much to benefit them, nobody else interested himself thus in their cause, fearless of the troubles he thereby drew down upon himself. He shared his goods with the poorest, slipped off his coat and gave it to the one who had none, and felt ashamed that he could leave his table satisfied when he knew many who had eaten nothing. He won the people's absolute confidence. They did not understand his odes, but his deeds were clear. They knew that here was a man who truly sought their welfare. And when he appeared as their teacher and adviser, they did not meet him with any of that suspicion which wonders why such a man should mix up in their affairs. Very soon "Henrik" became the universal helper in every possible adversity.

From personal observation both in the country and in the capital he had obtained a comprehensive knowledge of the general conditions and needs. In 1829 after a long tramp through the country he wrote the first volume of his occasional periodical for workmen, intended for publication in a widely distributed paper and circulated also among the population as a pamphlet issued by the royal society for the welfare of Norway. The zeal and enthusiasm that glow through this first address to the people remained just as ardent during his whole life. A second volume of the same

[53]

periodical was equally successful. It contained "encouragement to form societies in connection with the royal society for Norway's welfare." And in many parts of the country such local societies according to Wergeland's plan were in fact established for the economical and industrial progress of each parish. There was sound political wisdom in the central thought of this pamphlet, namely, that "liberty is a transient gift which easily escapes our grasp if we do not hold it fast in small units." Seven years later, after much struggle, this thought became politically valid in the law which established self-government in the parishes.

These papers for workmen he continued with some interruptions almost to the time of his death. In them he talked familiarly about all kinds of subjects—about drunkenness, cruelty to animals, superstition in one form or another, everything that pertained to the daily life of the poor. He did not hesitate to suggest even that the worst hovel could be made more attractive if a little paint were put on its walls or a few flowers placed in its windows. In such small practical ways he tried to raise the people's moral level, awaken their perception of beauty, and increase their comfort. Nor did he merely talk. Hosts of street arabs in the capital were his devoted friends and frequent visitors. He encouraged them to study, lent them books, examined them concerning the contents, made them read to him, got them situations—and all this in such a simple, winning way that he became at once their comrade and their idol whose praise they strove to win. He thus in many instances changed what might have been burdens on society into good and able citizens.

To Wergeland also belongs the credit of establishing public parish libraries. Beginning in his own circle, he had in a short time a loan library which he took care of himself. This example made an impression on the neighboring parishes. Numerous clergymen took up the idea, the government supported it, and thus not many years passed before each parish had its collection of books for general use. He planned, too, a "society for the enlightenment of the country population," a society whose members should give free instruction to young peasant boys and also make a yearly contribution toward the purchase of books for free distribution among the common people. It was not his fault that this plan was not realized till seventeen years later. At least he made the first effort himself by establishing a school in his own home where he taught Norwegian and geography. More than any other man he had learned from experience that if political activity is exercised by people too little versed in fundamental education, the result is danger to the state. In such cases (as in the United States) men cannot use to their true benefit the political power they have.

He was active also as a political speaker; and his speeches, illuminated as his practical ideas were with the glow of his poetical temperament, gave a true and perfect picture of his ideal of a Norwegian state. In one of them he beautifully reconciled the national with the universal when at the unveiling of a monument of a prominent patriot he said: "Like this column we will be Norwegian in our make-up, in speech, character, and grace; and yet, though keeping the glory of Norwegian citizenship, we will look full and wide into the world."

A question which occupied Wergeland for ten years or more was the admittance to Norway of Jews. The constitution refused them entrance. Not many occasions had arisen to act on the regulation, but there had been enough to arouse indignation among enlightened people; and at length the absurdity and inconsistency of such a measure in a constitution based on liberal and democratic principles were amply revealed. Norway had made her first state loan from a Jewish banking house in Hamburg. Now when in 1834 a new loan was to be negotiated, the necessary conference between the head of the Norwegian department of finance and the head of the Jewish bank could not take place till the government issued a letter of safe conduct for the Jew. It was valid for six weeks, but because of illness was not used. The government then had to issue another for the representative of the banking house, who was no less a personage than Salomon Heine, uncle of the famous German poet.

As the warm-hearted spokesman of religious tolerance and common sense, Wergeland rose up against such conditions and had an amendment proposed in the national assembly. He also vigorously advocated the cause in prose and verse. The amendment was supported by a host of the able and intelligent, and the best speakers defended it, even men who had opposed

Wergeland on other matters. But the measure did not get the necessary majority, owing to the votes of some of the clergy and many of the peasants. That was a disappointment to Wergeland—staunch friend of the peasants. But he kept up the contest. Among other things in defense of the cause he published a small collection of poems called *The Jew, Nine Blooming Branches from a Thornbush.* A little later came another, *The Jewess, Eleven Blooming Branches* etc. Even after a year's illness and after a second assembly had rejected the measure, his zeal was as warm and fresh as ever. Nothing gives better evidence of his enthusiastic interest in the cause than the poems just mentioned. They are political in a way, but the political element is united and fused with the most delicate, noble poetry. We cannot read *The Three* without being won by the grace with which tolerance is preached, and by the beauty and truthful coloring of the oriental life depicted, at once brilliant and naive. Who can help being inspired by the sad yet mild indignation of *The Wreck?* Or of *Moses on the Mountain?* And *Christmas Eve* surpasses them all in majesty and touching beauty.

Wergeland did not live to witness the victory. It was not gained till 1851, six years after his death. But he had done more for it than anybody, and even while the measure was still pending, the reward for his activity came from the gratitude of the excluded people. Before his countrymen could erect a monument in his honor, the Jews did it. In Sweden and

[57]

Denmark within the Jewish congregations money was raised for the purpose. The monument was unveiled in 1847 in Stockholm, because the contributors had as yet no access to Norway. With letters of safe conduct a deputation brought it to Christiania, where it was again unveiled in June 1849. Its face inscription is: "Henrik Wergeland, the tireless champion for men's and citizens' freedom and rights." On the reverse are the touching words: "Grateful Jews outside Norway erected this in his memory." A more beautiful and affecting memorial than this simple Gothic temple with its inscriptions no poet has ever received.

When one comes to speak of Wergeland just as a poet, one is tempted to say first of all that the place to think of him and approach him is not in a room, within walls that shut off our view, but out in the open air under the tent above and the traveling clouds— those "wonderlands of the sun"—whose praise he sang and to which his poetry may be likened: out among the woods and the meadows he loved and where he felt at home. For walls and doors do not suggest that spirit of freedom, that true human expansion, whose apostle he was. Beyond the expression of patriotic devotion—of which so much has here been said—and beyond the expression of general brotherhood and of human love, his poetry is above all a celebration of nature. The sun, the earth, the universe are to him constant sources of inspiration. His is a poetry whose richness of color and beauty of imagery can be equalled by few and surpassed by still fewer. To English-

Monument Given by Jews to Wergeland

speaking people Shakespeare represents the acme of enthusiastic language, the highest reach of splendor in glowing expression. And the same symphonic beauty of style, the same profusion of imagery and color are characteristic of Henrik Wergeland;—with the difference that his power is lyric rather than dramatic, and he applies his art to describe the world, the cosmos, rather than man, the microcosmos. Compared with his robust, many-colored sensuousness, the seraphic brilliancy of Shelley often grows pale and the ecstatic contemplation of Wordsworth didactic. The romantic age fostered such poets, worshippers of Nature, in which their souls were at liberty to ramble, ejaculating dithyrambs at every shrine, intoxicated with the magnificance of the great Vesture of Spirit. Wergeland, too, lies at the feet of Nature, yet not in a speculative or femininely sensitive or mystical attitude. He worships with the feeling of pure, jubilant youth, with enthusiasm glowing warm, and with a note of virility that most romanticists lack.

It is a sad fact for Norwegians that Wergeland's true position among the great poets of the world is not and perhaps cannot be generally understood: that we have to sing his praise to people incredulous because they have no means of knowing the facts or are too foreign to our national spirit to appreciate the character of his production. To put his work into translation would be as difficult as to translate the word-music of Swinburne and the spiritual suggestiveness of Tennyson. He himself had brief moments when he felt that the spirit of nationality to which he paid such ardent devotion was an idol that demanded too great sacrifices because it allowed him so meagre an audience. But such thoughts did not torment him long. He felt too strongly that in Norway he was needed and there was his proper field.

This lucid hope of his for everything good and just, this contented spirit, this unwearied buoyancy, will ever be one of the sources of his power. He is as fresh as a mountain wind, as pure and clear as a brook that dances over a rocky bed, coming from icy regions above, yet mirroring the beauty of the valley as it streams forth. Such gladness and strength, expressed in his inspired language, gladden us. With one master stroke the cobwebs of hesitation are swept from our troubled spirit—new springs of strength bubble up from secret depths within—the clouds of meditation sail gaily before the wind of new purpose—we are won again to serve our lifework with undimmed devotion. His fame today among his own people is as bright as ever, nay, even brighter. He is indeed an embodiment of the spirit of youth such as the nation loves to contemplate. His light has not been extinguished as has that of many contemporaries, but sparkles today from the uppermost height of our national firmament in undiminished glory and appealing beauty.

The huge epic of his youth, *Creation, Man, and Messias*, has never been much read, yet its ideas underlie everything Wergeland wrote later. Based on the Old and New Testaments, its three parts present the

Creation, the Aberration, and the Salvation of Man. The poem is full of exalted poetry and sentiment, and its ideas are those which for several generations had been leaving their impress upon European culture. In fact, it is the deism of the eighteenth century that finds expression in this account of universal history. The striving thought of that period in every direction is recognizable—Christianity seen as the gospel of the rights of man, philanthropy, liberalism tending toward republican government, hatred of oppressors and usurpers, socialistic utopias—all these are here expressed in positive poetical form. Yet the poet does not slip either into a pagan or a narrow Christian direction or into scepticism. Indeed, it is not too much to say that in this work is presented the best poetical summary in any literature of that eventful deistic movement in European thought. So representative is the poem of Wergeland's own ideas, that on his deathbed he rewrote it, convinced as much as ever of its value. Its basic idea was the constant inspiration of his whole life and activity. This idea is that the germ of perfection is present in the human race from the beginning, and though it may seem hidden or dormant for long periods, it is certain to revive, grow, and become triumphantly victorious in the end. But that idea is the basis of many shorter poems also, poems less philosophical and ambitious and more truly successful. It is on these that his fame and influence rest.

His finest political poem is *The Spaniard*, in which the cowardly policy of Ferdinand VII in the July

[61]

revolution is arraigned and the final victory of liberty warmly prophesied. There are magnificent lines in this poem and such description of the highlands of Norway as are found nowhere else in our literature.

A strange and characteristic work is *Jan van Huysum's Flowerpiece.* In this is the most complete expression of his myth-making tendency, his poet's habit of seeing the bee and the rose not merely as an insect and a flower but as endowed with souls like his own soul and able to enter into joyous communion with him.

His greatest, most magnificent poem, and one of his latest, is *The English Pilot.* Ill as he was when it was written, his impressions of the North Sea, the channel, and the luxuriant English nature are lived over again with a freshness and intensity of imagination fairly overwhelming. Such lavish splendor of natural scenery as Wergeland here produces no Norse poet has ever produced—not even he himself. Everything glitters and sparkles. It is not nature, but nature raised to its highest potency by a rich, glorious, poetical imagination. Within this wonderful wealth of natural scenery the story of the pilot is enclosed. We are shown the busy life of a powerful nation and historical memories attaching to that, civilization in its greatness and its corruption, the fresh life of the sailor at home and out in the world, the patriarchal happiness of homelife, nature in her grandeur and her innocence —all these elements are gathered and shaped in one supreme finished mould. Nowhere else did his poetical gifts find so broad a playground or reveal themselves thus in their fullness and variety.

The period from 1830 to 1845 is most significant in the history of our literature. It was a time when much old rubbish was cleared away, and many new things begun; a time of ferment and clashing opinions; of petty vanity, childish squabbles and coarse invective, and also of high thoughts, manly struggle, and the establishment of measures for growth in culture and power. Welhaven and his companions helped to make the time full of motion and contrast. Without them the period would not have had its clashing incidents, and the development would not have been so strong, so fruitful and so free from exaggeration. They contributed the criticism and purification which every intellectual movement needs. But the most prominent figure was and is Henrik Wergeland. He held this leading position not only because of his poetical genius but because in him was united all that moved the young Norway of the time;—its enthusiastic devotion to liberty and independence and its growing conception of a national culture. He was the young awakening Norway itself in all its early glory; stormy, fermenting, restless and active. He was this in every way—as political agitator and champion of liberty, as ultra-Norwegian, as popular teacher and philanthropist, and first and last as poet.

[The following remark is contributed by a Norwegian-American of repute. "During the national centenary celebration in 1914 Wergeland's grave was most beautifully decorated. Through the entire festivity he stood high above any other in the history of Norway. People veritably idolized him. He is universally called 'The Father of the Seventeenth of May.' In spite of all his faults he is and will remain the most beloved of Norse poets. Welhaven is more a master of style, but in depth of feeling he cannot approach Wergeland."—EDITOR.]

CAMILLA COLLETT

HAT wonderful power lies in a name! Especially in a dear and great name such as hers; a name made significant by her own unspoiled individuality. It is a nimbus; something indescribable about it forces us to pause and long observe it. Björnson has likened such a name to a constellation shining down upon us in peaceful, ever memorable greatness. But in Camilla Collett's name we are as much fascinated by the secret, the mysterious, as by the transparent and clear. We think of winged flight, of the song of hidden birds, of the gentle falling of white cherry petals. The charm of the mountain nymph rests on this name. It reminds us of the leafy woods, the river bank lying amid alder and hazel, and the silent occult spirit-haunted life of the woods of Norway.

She was perhaps the most characteristic phenomenon in our history—this clergyman's daughter from Eidsvold, who became our greatest authoress and our valkyrie, who for more than a generation in a little corner of the world carried on the struggle for the rights of the woman-heart, of the human soul, against the power of all conventionalities and customs and fought it with triumph. Yet with all her ideal courage and her ire, she remained the same shy, reserved person as

in her youth, the same mimosa in the presence of outsiders, especially of the great public, which repelled
her by its obtrusion, its lack of regard for talent other
than amusing, its indifference to the mental real values.
But many a mother and father, many a young girl
and boy, read what she wrote and imbibed strength to
defend, to strike a blow for worth, to prevent the flower
of existence from being trodden under foot. Thus she
lived among us year by year, unknown to the multitude,
hidden from the masses, forgotten by many, until she
felt her existence too cramped, too pallid and deathlike,
and withdrew abroad to surroundings which better
suited her nature. There among artists and authors
and their works she breathed the free air of eternal
ideas and great accomplishments. Self-exiled thus as
she was, she nevertheless continued to bring to her
native land the fruits of her thoughts, her work, and
her struggle.

It is now a hundred years since Camilla Collett was
born. The history of her life has been written by her
son, a fascinating book which makes him, who wrote it,
and her, who inspired it, almost equally great. Unaf-
fected and unostentatious as herself, it tells in a big
clear way, mostly in her own words, the story of her
development. Her career was in the best sense free
from blemish, her speech as pure as her thoughts. She
was not ignorant of the shady side of existence, but she
abhorred all things questionable, gossip, and foulness.
None of these penetrated her life or her books. Her
greatest work, *The Daughters of the County Magis-*

trate, has few parallels in any literature. It was the child of her sorrows, and it is a sorrowful book; yet it is so exceedingly charming, so beautiful in tone, so delicate in feeling, so artistically moulded and balanced, so elevated, so powerful in its pathos, as to be almost alone in its kind. Of all the books I have read I can scarcely recollect any that made such an ineffaceable impression upon me. If any, perhaps those of Turgenieff, with whom indeed Fru Collett has much in common, in viewpoint and manner and incomparable mastery of language. Yet there is a difference. While he in sad resignation seems to say: "Well, the world is not any better," she with wrath dissolved in irony exclaims: "Beyond all criticism, the world is absurd!"

Fru Collett's work for women's rights laid the nation under great obligation to her, and for this she has also been greatly praised. Though a true aristocrat, she was also a true democrat in disposition, and was in her lifework equally near to the highest and the lowest. Quite as much as her brother, Henrik Wergeland, she was a popular poet, a friend of the people, and a patriot. For though she might have affiliated with Danish, German, or French interests and become prominent in them, it was after all the Norwegian women that she aroused and whose prophetess she became. In recognition of this great patriotic work, perhaps more than because she was a notable author and master of language, her statue was erected in Christiania—an occasion marked by a festivity in which even King Haakon and Queen Maud did homage to this queen of genius as

she stood there in bronze, still chilled, still brooding, as
in life, but lifted above the variable weather of the day
and the times.

Perhaps a word of personal recollection will be par-
doned me. I knew Fru Collett even when I was a
little girl. For many years my mother took me along
to pay her visits. She had then as a rule no home of
her own. Her sons were out in the world and she herself preferred to come and go as weather and mood
dictated. I was fortunate enough to have in my mother
a mentor who could enlighten my youthful ignorance
and tell me about Fru Collett's younger days when she
had been the charming Camilla Wergeland, the
unequalled beauty of Christiania; and later when as a
widow she strove to reach the unattainable in such
social conditions as ours then were. There was much
in the story to fill the heart with compassion for the
fine flower whose plumules life's inclement blast had
shriveled. My mother was very fond of Fru Collett.
Fate had not been lenient, and Fru Collett had helped
when there was most dire need. In that way I came to
regard her with admiring deference. Her relationship
to me was distant, yet she was much nearer to my
heart than any of my other relatives. I remember her
best in her seventies, a slender stooped figure that
moved about lightly with an individual charm and
spoke in a soft rather veiled voice. At times indeed
she became resentful, proudly straightening up and
gesticulating violently. The pale face was by this time
furrowed and the eyes deeply sunken, but the forehead

was high and mighty and the straight-combed hair was venerable.

We always brought her some dainties, especially cakes, of which she was very fond, and she served wine in return. She was exceedingly near-sighted, and fumbled about for her glasses if she had mislaid them, but her eyes were not lifeless, as near-sighted eyes often are. On the contrary, they shone with an unusual heaven-blue sheen, almost like Grieg's, when she became interested and something joyous warmed her sensitive soul. Then she suddenly grew fifty years younger, animated and overbubbling. She was jocular and witty, and her remarks had that peculiar "esprit" which is both merry and significant. Indeed, she was a fine instrument which only a skilled hand could play, but when such a hand touched her, she gave resonance for every motion, both in melody and chord.

Generous she was almost to a fault, yet without the least ostentation, never mentioning her small kindnesses. There was always a five or a ten crown bill under the lamp or the inkwell which she almost forced on her visitor if she thought it was needed. And if she did not immediately find what she was seeking, she rustled about in a drawer and brought out something she had recently bought on a journey or had long kept intending to gladden the heart of one or another of her friends. It was the poor and the lowly who appreciated her and who unmistakably showed their feeling, just as they did for her brother. The great and the mighty, in her lifetime, too often passed her by,

The last time I saw her was in Copenhagen. I had just won my doctor's degree at Zürich, but my mother had died while I was away and all the drudgery seemed of little use. Neither of us could say much, both struggled to keep back the tears. But she praised me more than anyone else did for being the leader in such an attainment, and she asked questions about my studies and was almost deferential toward my little achievement. But thus she was always—full of enthusiasm and joy over the accomplishments of others, especially if they were women who had reached thus some success. It was during this visit that she said that when I went to America I could perhaps make her known over there. At the time I did not have much hope of accomplishing anything in the world; my plans seemed almost ruined, and I replied quite evasively. But I have often thought about my answer and regretted it. She so rarely asked favors, and when she did there was so often something to hinder. Now she had again been met, and by me, with apparent unwillingness. And this is why with special pleasure I tell through the following translation something more in detail of her life and work.

A Sketch of Camilla Collett*

"When were ever diamonds ponderous? While common graystone may be mountains wondrous."

These words of her great brother might be properly placed as the motto of Fru Collett's literary activity.

*Translated and arranged by A. M. W. from the Norwegian of Mathilde Schjött, in *Norway During the Nineteenth Century.*

The brilliance, firmness, purity, and beauty of her style—its diamondlike quality—is what decides her high rank as a writer. By virtue of this, her books, though few, withstand the influence of time and her name retains its lustre undimmed by the greatness of later authors. Fru Aubert in a late book says truly that mighty geniuses known by all the world have since enriched our literature; but hardly any creative work has so revolutionized minds as did Fru Collett's *The Daughters of the County Magistrate.* And with the assurance of one who lived through the period she declares, "The book had this power because it was Norwegian, because it began a new form of activity in our social development, and because it was expressed in a style which after fifty years remains unsurpassed in our literature."

Many things contributed to make Camilla Collett remarkable. She was born in 1813, that is to say, she grew up with our lately regained independence, at a time when much that was old and retrogressive was cut away and much that was new was brought into being. And she grew up at Eidsvold, the garden spot, the seed-ground of the new freedom, where the new conditions sprang into life. She was the daughter of Nicolai Wergeland and the sister of Henrik Wergeland— this means that she lived among powerful personalities who each in his way helped to tear apart as well as to build up, who stood in the midst of conflicts, among the foremost leaders in the struggle, bringing to an issue matters of life and death to the nation, and who

Nicolai and Alette Wergeland

were also themselves an issue in the controversy. No wonder that she too received the latent elements of a combative nature; that she too, while suffering from the fray and for a time oppressed and cowed by it, later developed those seeds of contention and ended by raising in her own sphere a controversy between life and death and becoming in her turn an issue in the controversy.

Even her parents represented contrasts within the same society. The father, Nicolai Wergeland, was a gifted boy of peasant stock, and with melancholy ardor recognized in himself all kinds of possibilities and competencies, which largely by his own exertions he developed through all stages till he reached the height of the culture of his day. The mother, on the other hand, was a fair accomplished daughter of an artistically gifted family, complete in its refinement and intellectual development. Old breeding, fresh ability —such is the union from which the greatest minds and choicest spirits have arisen. But perhaps it is also the source of much contradiction of qualities, much distress, much innate capacity for suffering. Fru Collett received her full share of this painful endowment. While her brother could say, "Surely from the mother doth the son inherit heart," and seemed to have received his mother's lightsome, easy, unreflective, and elastic temperament, Fru Collett inherited her father's trait of melancholy brooding, much of his heaviness of mood and inelastic spirit, but also his logical reflective mind and his deep feeling. On the other hand, it is true that while Henrik Wergeland's talent seems to have gone back to his father's unspoiled vigor with all its crudeness, presenting at first but a chaos of possibilities and having to pass through many processes before it reached its maturity and perfection, his sister was born with a perfect sense of art and form and with a precociousness of taste peculiar to highly cultured natures.

After severe studies and brilliant examinations, Nicolai Wergeland settled in Christiansand as assistant teacher in the Latin School and afterwards resident curate. He married in 1807 the lovely and beautiful Alette Thaulow. For ten happy years they remained in Christiansand; he prominent as a teacher and preacher, also as a writer, his dissertation on a Norwegian University especially creating a stir. Both husband and wife were brilliant in the society life of the wealthy vivacious busy town, and not least in amateur comedy because of their dramatic talent. Of their children, all born in Christiansand, the eldest was Henrik and the youngest but one Jacobine Camilla. She was named after one of the dramatic parts in which the mother had scored her greatest triumphs.

Nicolai Wergeland was sufficiently a man of mark to be sent as delegate to the National Assembly at Eidsvold called to consider the results of the separation from Denmark, and he soon became one of the leaders as well as one of the most discussed persons there. While in this beautiful region, the thought was born in him of applying for the living at Eidsvold when it

Eidsvold Parsonage

should become vacant. To be pastor far off in the Eastland had always been his aim as a boy; to work among the "unspoiled country people" seemed to him a most engaging prospect.

The living fell vacant and he got it. The reality, however, was not so full of charm as he and his lovely wife had pictured it. He had seen the Manse first in its festive garb, full of people and decorated to receive princes and delegates. The second time he found it empty and half tumbledown. Nor were the conditions among the "unspoiled country people" so idyllic as he had expected. The daughter in her writings refers to conditions which filled her with horror. The mother had to begin housekeeping on a scale hitherto unknown and to deal with many coarse and rude people. Indeed, in the first years the family endured much. The mother probably never overcame the sense of homesickness for those she had left in Christiansand. The father entered with energy into his duties and the needs of the farm. Diversion was found in the beautiful surroundings, beloved by both. The taste for reading was easily satisfied by the pastor's large library, and once in a long while the advent of a visitor did its share to mitigate the languors of solitude.

"The closed paradise of childhood, the purgatory of boarding school, the dizzy dream of youth, the ordeal of practical life—thus Fru Collett in her novel, *The Manor*, characterizes the stage, through which a young woman's life passes from its quiet budding till it bursts forth either to bear flowers or to wither. To her, Eidsvold was this closed paradise of childhood. The parsonage itself was seigneurial and stately in character, with large rooms, high windows, broad easy stairs, and long dark halls, where sometimes, indeed, in black stormy nights the wind boomed unpleasantly. In front was a large open yard and farther away were the outhouses. There gathered all the establishment could harbor of two and four-legged animals. What greater joy could there be for a child! The whole family loved animals and each had one or more pets. When a kid was to be killed, both mother and daughter wept; the mother every day fed from her window Henrik's pony; the daughter had a favorite cat which followed her everywhere. The bellwether helped himself undismayed to the moss roses, carefully cherished by both mother and daughter in anticipation of visitors from Christiania. The billygoat solemnly stalked through the hall into the dining-room and broke the severe decorum of the meals. The occupations of a big household also proved interesting to a little girl. There were bakings, brewings, weaving, spinning, conserving, as well as killing of the fat of the land. Everywhere was she present as attentive spectator.

But the best of all was the outdoor life—an incessant sporting in the open air. "Fortunately," says she, "neither of our parents had any of that untimely anxiety with which some mothers think to protect a child, while instead of preventing dangers, they invite them and make the child defenseless against them. To us was given every opportunity to become practiced and hardened." And they made good use of their opportunity. The place was full of steeps, ravines, dams and rivers. They walked the railing of the bridges, they jumped through a whole story down on an armful of hay not larger than a man might carry into a manger. How many times they plumped into the river and saved themselves by clutching the weeds, she cannot recollect. Their most dangerous amusement was to go exactly to the point beyond which the current catches the boat and hurls it toward the cataracts. We are but too willing to believe that they became adroit and hardy and accustomed to enduring pain. Here is an instance. When nine years of age she sledged with her three-year old brother in her lap on an ice-covered road through a long winding valley. He escaped unhurt; but she came home with a gash in her temple and a closed eye. In this condition she seated herself at Lisbeth's spinning-wheel and spun—as a joking surprise to the nurse.

This same Lisbeth plays a beautiful part in that secluded paradise of childhood. She was a nurse such as is seldom found, and she was not without influence on the poetic gift developed in the two children. Lisbeth was the daughter of "Sara with the wooden nose" whose history Fru Collett tells so touchingly. Sara knew all sorts of fairy stories—Norwegian, Spanish, French, Arabian. She seldom told them to outsiders, but she deposited the whole of her wealth with her daughter. In that mother's humble cabin watergruel was the fare morning, noon, and night. The only break

in it was when there was no more to be had. On such
evenings when they had nothing to eat, the mother told
fairy stories and hunger was forgotten in the romance
of bewitched castles and the glories of "The Thousand
and One Nights." "Oh, this daughter must have gone
hungry often," exclaims Fru Collett, "for she knew
many fairy stories. I need give no more impressive
evidence of her great gift than that for ten long years
she had the task of feeding a brood of children as
greedy and eager for fairy tales as are the swallow's
young for worms. And so marvelously did she satisfy
the quest that we always believed we heard something
new even when she was only retelling the old."

The housekeeper, too, the mirthful Dorothea Bay,
contributed to their poetic education. She had at her
command almost the whole range of songs and ditties,
known and unknown, old and new. Among them were
especially those of Bellman, at that time extremely
popular; and to the children's unbounded delight, she
occasionally warbled them forth.

Real instruction was given by tutors chosen from
among the least incapable and unbearable of their kind.
As the daughter shared the brothers' open-air life, so
she also participated in their studies. Fortunately the
father superintended the instruction and undertook
even to teach some of the subjects. Fru Collett says
of his teaching: "The most obscure became compre-
hensible, the dryest became interesting and instructive.
We never felt weariness but thought we had just had a
good time." The father's educational venture, how-

ever, was not restricted to book learning. He watched severely over their behavior and propriety of manner. They loved him and wooed him in order to obtain from him a smile, a mark of approval; if they found anything rare, the first berry or the first flower, they brought it to him rather than to the mother. "Praise from him had a special flavor and was more difficult to obtain." But they were also afraid of him. "When we heard his slow ponderous step on the stairs, play no less than strife ceased and the room assumed an aspect of peace. Mother threw a glance around to see if perhaps a chair or table had changed place. Woe to the one who was not well-mannered at table, who came late to meals, or otherwise offended against the ceremonial. The nursery was next to father's room upstairs, so that he had us completely under his eye. It was all right for us to play and especially sing, of that he never had too much. But all noise and other discord was at once stopped by a sign from within. If to cap the climax he showed his serious face at the door, the room became as silent as a church." On the other hand, if anything was the matter with them he was all concern, sat by the bedside, sang for them, and watched with them. And his great gifts as a social leader he did not consider too precious to be used for the pleasure of his home. Birthdays were made occasions of much rejoicing, and of the children's games he was the very soul; especially the conundrums or written games became amusing and piquant only when he took part in them. It was characteristic of this home that complaints or unpleasant remarks or showing visitors anything but a friendly manner were strictly, though quietly, forbidden. This last enforcement is especially significant. It suggests a time of pell mell hospitality when many wrecked and homeless wanderers were drifting wherever they might find the least sign of welcome. It also pictures the parsonage as a place where such eccentrics were looked upon as real rare-bits, literally dragged to the house by that admirer of eccentrics, Henrik Wergeland, himself the most eccentric of them all.

The mother had by nature the friendliness and gentle pity that make rules superfluous. She was courtesy embodied and sought always with the greatest leniency to accommodate herself to the demands of country hospitality as then existing, and put up as cheerfully as she might with whatever Providence bestowed in the form of guests, evil or good. It is a lovely portrait Fru Collett draws of her mother—a child's spirit, a seraph's heart, preserving to the last a young girl's delicacy of feeling and shyness; light as a bird in her movements and walk, with noble, almost royal features. She did everything with incomparable quickness; when sewing or knitting it was impossible to follow the rapid movements of her fingers. She was domestic and industrious; whether she was practical in the sense of having something besides knowledge of details, the daughter dares not say, but it was always good to be near her.

II

The brothers and a cousin who was educated with them left after a time for the capital to enter school. Camilla saw them now only in vacation, and regular schooling for her ceased. One or two studies she still pursued under her father's direction. But alone she read much more. She had a passion for reading and plenty of opportunity to satisfy it. Besides this pleasure, she had the delight of free roaming in the woods. For half a day at a time she was often there with only Nature to bear her company. "It was then that I became a poet," says George Sand, speaking of her lonely childhood and early youth in the woods and fields. It was likewise with Fru Collett. The introspective trait in her character as well as her sympathetic identification of herself with the moods of Nature were active then, and were joined with the capacity— so fatal to one's happiness—of retaining and brooding over past impressions and feelings. "Of the solitude," she says, "which reigned in these valleys and along the deep winding river, one can now form no idea. What thoughts, plans, dreams, have these valleys not given birth to!" And she remembers what indescribable sadness overcame her "especially during the long Sunday afternoons when spring was breaking forth with sunshine and ice-cold wind, when the colt's-foot sprouted in the clay and the birches bled from the wounds we inflicted on them."

Meanwhile the thoughtful teacher, her father, made up his mind that regular instruction together with girls of her own age might be helpful to his daughter, and from her fourteenth year to her completed six-teenth she had to pass through the "purgatory of the boarding school." With the exception of a little book-learning, which she had absorbed in direct ratio to her liking for those who taught it, she came out of school as wise as she went in—just as shy, confused, and unsettled; unfit to begin life as it was, she says herself. But she concedes one thing—she took away with her a treasure of happy impressions which she could never be wholly deprived of. She had there met people so excellent, of their kind so perfect, that the mere memory had restorative power when she was near losing faith in humanity, and proved a remedy against the dire conception later in vogue of the human soul as a cess-pool of sin and iniquity.

When she returned, her father, after careful prepa-rations, confirmed her. And then began what she has so many times called her "long youth." One thing is at once evident. The bold, brave, gay outdoor life with the boys was over. She who so many times had risked her life together with them, who burned to do something, now sat by the pond and watched her broth-ers skate, suffering the tortures of Tantalus from desire to join, but could not. Was she lame or injured? Not at all. She merely did not dare. She had become subject to the stern law of womanliness. Her mother, now that she was a young girl, feared that she should make herself conspicuous (on a pond in the country!) and was strongly upheld by a sister. A grandaunt

[80]

had once said, "The woman who is least spoken of is always the best," and this word passed down the generations as a family motto. Camilla Wergeland herself took the warning so to heart that not even "the most rigorous English society rules, which can boast of having ushered prudery into the world, could find anything to object to." The result was that "from being a lively child she became as silent and reserved a young girl as ever bored herself and others by playing the sphinx." During her "long youth" she moved among an army of "don'ts" as if in a dance upon eggs.

She had also another passion—to act. It was indeed innate in her. It drew nourishment from the very sound of her name, from memories of her childhood, from everything connected with Christiansand, from the mother's own youth. But her theatrical propensities met no encouragement. In her book called *The Long Nights* she says (Ninth Night), "Yes, me too the tragic muse kissed when I lay in the cradle, and she loved me and willed me a considerable legacy. I can tell you this, my listeners, with the same proud rich man's sensation that a beggarly fellow has in speaking of the inheritance he surely once owned but lost in a lawsuit. . . . I lost my lawsuit, I lost it before the narrow-minded barrier called 'family consideration,' where many consecrated artist souls have lost their case. I lost the legacy of my muse, but her kiss burned long, long upon my forehead, and at times I feel it still. . . . I still acknowledge this art to

[81]

be the form in which my strongest individual life would most naturally have found its expression."

Why did she submit? The mother's authority alone could not decide her. She submitted because times were different then, and because at the present stage of her development these demands of propriety and heroic self-sacrifice met a responsive chord in herself. But the deepest cause was after all the shyness and timidity which solitude had produced in her. To oppose prejudices did not come to her mind. She did not even plead her cause but without a sound allowed herself to be "throttled." If she had been intrepid, if she had skated, continued the jolly free life with her brothers, if she had followed the promptings of her muse and become an actress—"If only she had . . . . . if only she had not . . . . ." Such are the regrets that surrounded the fate of the young girl in *The Daughters of the Country Magistrate.*

But if she had, Fru Collett would not have been what she was. Her character would not have remained so shy and sensitive, so crystal clear, her feeling for the oppressed would not have been so sympathetic, so quick to detect wrong; and her struggle would not have been so powerful as it came to be when under long pressure it had developed far into the very depths of her being. Nor would her awakening have been so complete.

Camilla Wergeland

III

Her horizon, however, was not confined to Eidsvold. The city, that is Christiania, was the object of her desire. "The city, that was life, that was the world, that was fate." But the city was far away—then. The journey was twelve Norwegian miles (some seventy English) if not more; the road was stony and hilly where it was not bottomless sand. The logdrivers with their rows of sledges blocked the passage for travelers and by their roars of "half way" drove them nearly or wholly into the ditch. The relay stations were something dreadful, yet if the carriage broke down, as often happened "on the eighth hill," one might be compelled to accept with thankfulness a lodging for the night. Nevertheless in later years the memory of these first trips to the city seemed "bright and fair." They became yearly visits and began when she was between sixteen and seventeen years old.

It must be counted as evidence of Fru Collett's tact and taste that she hardly ever spoke of her own appearance, still less of her positive personal beauty. And yet this beauty certainly played a great part in her life, unconsciously to herself determining her demands and expectations. But this silence is retrieved by what others have told about her. The rumor of her exquisite beauty still hovers around her name like a golden cloud. "The lightsome elf of sixteen years . . . . . fostered in the deep valleys" is one comment. "To see her enter a ballroom was something quite unusual." "She seemed like a revelation such as nature sometimes offers us, the airy mist of morning gliding along a mountain side, or moonlight delicately playing on the water." Thus opinions all agree in giving an impression of something rare, not wholly of this world.

In the city Camilla Wergeland met the poet Welhaven, and with him passed through what she called "the dizzy dream of youth." Fru Collett has several times written of Welhaven, but in a wholly dispassionate, objective way. That she knew him personally, that she stood close to him, is not even hinted—an attitude characteristic of her and of the age in which she lived. But it has been supposed that below the veil of poetry Welhaven's image may be found in her writings; as in the beautiful passage in *The Long Nights* where the description of nature's mood leads up to and emphasizes the incident of the little pink letter which when she had read it and it had slipped down on the sand, looked as innocent as a petal fallen with others from the blooming apple tree. "And yet it had been weighty enough to crush a hope for life." The powerful and touching poem, *Before the Gates of Death*, seems to have been an outburst beyond control; none the less so because the confession suddenly breaks off, sealed with eternal muteness.

When the two first met, each made a deep impression on the other. In a poem Welhaven says of her, "Most plain, though least comprehended, was her noble yet simple sway of souls. She stood with an invisible crown amid this festive throng, for on her alone rested the

Welhaven

lustre of pure and sweet womanhood." The homage
of the poem he strengthened by personal homage and
found willing assistants among her friends. Camilla
Wergeland, however, was so retiring, so unapproach-
able, that it was difficult to bring about any closer
acquaintance. The very attraction she felt made her
avoid him.

During these years (the thirties) the strife between
Henrik Wergeland and Welhaven, half political and
half literary, was very bitter indeed, and their adherents shared their antagonism. To some of them a war
on paper was not sufficient. Welhaven, as the one who
represented the opposition to the commoners, suffered
most. Stones were hurled after him in the streets. A
man who looked like him was one evening assailed and
brutally beaten. Camilla Wergeland's whole disposition drew her to Welhaven's side; it would not have
been necessary for her first to entertain any personal
interest in him. That he was persecuted by her brother's adherents and, as it were, in his name, could only
increase her anger and pain. She openly expressed
her indignation at the treatment Welhaven underwent,
and she and her friend Emilie Diriks named him Saint
Sebastian. He heard of this and wrote a reverential
letter wherein the pleasure of addressing her and knowing that she understood him quivered beneath the
pedantic form. He disarmed and mollified her surprise
at so strange a step by presupposing that it must be
surprising and accepted the name with which she had
so flattered him. Thus the ice was broken, at least

[85]

in part, and they entered into a more natural relation. They could now speak "gently and calmly" to each other and enjoy their "souls' harmony." The correspondence was continued, the acquaintance progressed into a delicate secret understanding, a relation without name or aim, on a dizzy verge between love and friendship, to which they tried to give firmness by a brother and sister relation. Through poems and letters it is possible to follow the stages. They were together under the lindentree "while the lark sang in the cloudless sky of the beating of their hearts." She played for him and on "the gently soaring tones their hearts met." But even now the mood was sadness, they were "rocked in the lap of pensiveness" and felt "with nameless trembling that the first bloom of tenderness was to waste away in brooding regret."

Why this contradiction, grief, and doubt? Why could a young man not hold and bind to himself a heart that was his? Was it his complete lack of worldly position and prospects? Was it his antagonism to her brother which after all brought discord? Or was it lack of courage on his part—a thing not uncommon—lack of courage to live up to his choice,—or possibly courage of another kind? Did he need to be cheered, to be met on the way, as she with her reserved nature could not meet him? "Strangely and mightily was I drawn to you as to something far off and mysterious," he says in a letter many years later, "and you were always remote, on flight, absent, even when present and despite the harmony of our souls." Were they both too much

alike, too shy, too cool, to melt thoroughly together?
Their correspondence seems to indicate this. One who
knew both of them well declared, "Welhaven was himself embarrassed and timid in spite of his challenging
manner. He needed that one should meet him half
way. Camilla was always shy, always retiring. Ida
Kjerulf came and gave him the look which is at once
tender and certain."

Years afterwards (1876) Fru Collett wrote an article
relative to Ibsen's *Comedy of Love* which had just
been played in Christiania. The article is very objective in tone, treats only of Ibsen's play, but as the
story of Welhaven and Camilla Wergeland was scarcely
absent from Ibsen's thought, so Fru Collett's remarks
on the play unconsciously reveal her own feelings
and experiences. In the light—one might say in
the shelter—of Ibsen's play Fru Collett sees her own
youth as such a comedy of love; and although she
does not betray herself even by a flutter of the eye-
lids, it is from the judgment-seat of her own practical
wisdom that she passes sentence on the relation of
which Ibsen's play treats. She says, "We must all
agree that sympathy of souls, a more ideal view of
life entertained by both partners, is what makes a marriage, as Ibsen implies, a union in truth." But she
shows how Ibsen's satire on soulless marriage misses
its aim and hits all marriage, the institution as such;
"otherwise marriage would be sanctioned by the union
of the two lovers Svanhild and Falk. But although
in them the ideal seems to be reached and nothing from

[87]

outside prevents the union, they separate of their own free will. We say although—should we say *because* the conditions are ideal, they make their escape? That is Ibsen's secret." She goes on to describe the way relations such as Falk's to Svanhild end in our society. "When these falcons (Falk means falcon) have played idealist for awhile with their victims, they grow weary of the game and let the half plucked dove lie, a prey to grief or to some chance rescuer not at all of the ideal kind." And what if instead of dove we put the word woman? "Her freshness of heart is nipped in the bud, her capacity for happiness sadly reduced." Falk's refrain:

> "I broke the flower, little it matters
> Who gets the dead remains,"

is to Fru Collett the chief thing in the play. In other words, pained irony is the feeling she expresses at having allowed herself to be dazzled and blinded by the game of ideal sentiment. Unexpected, quick as the stroke of a whip follows the closing sentence of the keen little article. "Why do Falk and Svanhild so heroically abstain from marrying? I shall whisper it in your ear, reader, but do not betray me. Because . . . they loved each other . . . *never!*"

Again, many years later (1887) in a preface relating to that irrevocable epoch in life when one faces one's *either—or*, she says, "Quietly, almost bereft of will power, did she let life and happiness pass by, dared not grasp, dared not lay hold of either. And life and happiness must be grasped, must be held fast; they

beckon merely and disappear." Thus she saw this
event differently according to her mood. At times it
seemed to her as if he had burned up her youth in
incense before himself. At other times she saw the whole
matter as a calamity the cause of which lay as much
in her as in him. And at last—this is what her intimate
friends say—the bitterness went away, she became
reconciled and there remained only the proud memory
of a glorious youth.

IV

As everybody knows, the poetic sorrow which Welhaven had infused into his relation to Camilla Wergeland became his in fullest measure in his relation to
Ida Kjerulf. Her parents strenuously opposed their
union, and it was only after several years of suffering
and when Ida Kjerulf was doomed by consumption that
Welhaven was allowed to come freely and see her. She
died in September, 1840. This grief brought to Welhaven's poems that tone which makes him the poet of
those who know sorrow. The one who pitied him most
sincerely and deeply and who understood his woe and
the effect of it on his character—while others took
offence at his manner of expressing his bereavement—
was Camilla Wergeland. Not that her sympathy ever
reached him; it was felt only by those who presumed
to be his critics.

Meanwhile Camilla Wergeland had found a knight,
a rescuer, far superior to Gulstad in the *Comedy of
Love* and even to the splendid Dean in *The Magis-*

trate's Daughters. Jonas Collett belonged to one of the oldest and best families in Christiania. Of him it is rightly said that he needed no dubbing to be a nobleman. Prominent as a jurist, he was also a keen student and critic of literature and as such was highly regarded by his contemporaries. In many places in her works Fru Collett has made touching and grateful mention of him. Some of her remarks show how downcast she felt after her heart's "mortal agony" with which her long youth ended. "He raised the half perishing one," she says, "and placed her by his side. He inquired lovingly into her whole state and told her there was yet much to be saved. Yea, it was he who gave the oppressed courage, who freed her mind and gave her back speech, he it was who made a true human being of her." From the fantastically disguised but no doubt genuine correspondence in *The Long Nights* (between Ernest and Helen), it is evident that for a long while she resisted. She considered herself too old—through with life. But Collett was not afraid. He was a man who "felt able to bear even the biggest burden on earth, a lonely, proud, wounded heart," and able to "dispel the sorcery under which the princess of his heart had been pining." And she gave in and bound herself to him.

While they were engaged, Collett on a public stipend made a trip to Italy. His letters to her (printed in *Ydale* in 1851) can be read with great interest, written as they were by one before whose cultured taste and refined appreciation Italy revealed her treasures,

Fru Collett about 1841

and addressed to the one to whom he offered only his best. Thus indirectly she came to share in the journey. After his return and his appointment as lecturer on jurisprudence, they were married, July 14, 1841. On her marriage she entered that next stage in her development which she calls "the ordeal of practical life."

Jörgen Moe, in his obituary on Collett, made charming mention of the hospitality of their home. "The circle that frequented it was not large," he says, "but those who entered it enjoyed most refreshing hours, strengthening to the spirit." He praises the clearness characteristic of Collett's conversation and his great charm. "But to be sure," he adds, "Collett was one of the few who in his home could speak of the highest and best with certainty of being understood"—a handsome compliment to the wife; and even in this discreet form extraordinary at a time when it was almost chivalrous to keep women out of conversation, not to mention print. Asbjörnsen* also, the other great leader in the new national interest in the native folk poetry, came to Collett's.

It is almost imperative to have been in touch with people of that time to understand the enthusiasm which greeted that awakening of the nation to the value of its own poetical lore; to realize how many helped, how much individual initiative, independence, and spontane-

*Jörgen Moe and Asbjörnsen published the first extensive collection of Norse fairy tales and folk stories. They are to Norway what Hans Christian Anderson is to Denmark. See Note on Welhaven, p. 102.—ED.

ous effort were displayed. Fru Collett—who sat there with her treasure of fairy stories all prepared, to whom the "elfins of the woods had whispered the wonderful" —naturally became one of the first to participate. Asbjörnsen found in her both a collaborator and a source. His feuilleton *Bird Song and Fairy Blood*, published in *The Constitutional* in 1843, he says was the first thing that awakened the interest she afterwards showed in his writings. To and for Asbjörnsen the next year she wrote *By the Drake River*. There she introduces the best teller of stories the parish could produce, the excellent nurse Lisbeth, and makes her tell him her best story—*The Story of the Desert Princess*, the Norse version of the Greek Psyche legend. And Asbjörnsen met Anna Maria (as he called Lisbeth) and got from her a number of tales and fairy stories, and was besides referred to Sexton Peter at Eidsvold Church as a veritable treasure trove for such matters. But Sexton Peter—who should know his situation and the locality better than Fru Collett? Hence she wrote for Asbjörnsen the greater part of the Introduction to *The Sexton's Tales*, and also the opening sentences of *From Mountain and Dairy Farm*, which are also laid at Eidsvold.

All this assistance was at first at Collett's express desire kept perfectly secret, the chief reason being Fru Collett's own shrinking from publicity; and it was never mentioned by her. Meanwhile Collett, whether or not with conscious intention is hard to say, mentally prepared her to come forward as an author.

The next step was to do it practically. She tells us that Collett, aside from his special line, had very little time to read. Hence he appointed her to select what was worth while in the literary productions of the day and report on them. She was not to read to him, but to tell him from what she had read. In this way on promenades back and forth on the floor in the evenings a new novel by Gutzkow or Sternberg was in the briefest possible fashion appropriated, sifted, and discussed. She was proud of this new position. And once when she was at Eidsvold on a summer visit, he wrote her that Munch had begged a feuilleton of him—would she not please write it? At first he met energetic protest; then she did it by taking a description he had sent her of a day at Eidsvold, continuing and completing it. The fusion was perfect. Afterward some lesser pieces came, *The Manor* in *At Home and Abroad* (1847), and *An Encounter* (printed in *Ydale*, 1851). Both were laid at Eidsvold, and both appeared anonymously;—an anonymity "sealed with seven seals," which, however, did not mislead anyone. In the same *Ydale* appeared Collett's letters from Rome. Thus husband and wife appeared together, for the first and also for the last time.

During the ten years of Fru Collett's marriage, death had several times broken into her circle. In 1843 her mother died. Days of gloom hard to bear had come to the parsonage. Her father had not been considered in the appointment of a new bishop for Christiansand, and the hope of the parents of ending their days in the dear old place came thus to naught. After this disappointment the mother faded away into death almost without illness. Two years afterwards came the close of Henrik Wergeland's short life, and in 1848 her father passed away. But in 1851 came the great blow. Collett died. He had never been so strong as might be desired, yet death came unexpectedly after a short illness. In *The Long Nights* we are told, "There was one who would not believe it, who passed the night brooding over whether it was really true; and this solitary one—you know who it was. Two alone on an island in the great empty sea—one is left behind; how is it possible to understand such a thing?"

When Collett died, it seemed as if her first timid steps on the path of literary endeavor were to be also the last. "It was as if I could not be anything alone," she helplessly exclaims. But in fact she found her salvation in continuing on the road where he had guided her. She now began *The Daughters of the County Magistrate,* and completed the first part in 1853, the second in 1855. The sensation caused by the book is a matter of common knowledge. "How well one knew it all, and yet how fresh and kindling the idea! Who can ever forget it?" says Fru Aubert. The author showed a first hand knowledge of the situation treated, the persons were drawn with an acute sense of their peculiarities, made alive and different; the conversations were dramatic; nature was described as only a true worshipper can describe it; and above all there was true and deep feeling, never prolix, but with fine restraint

[94]

seeking its contrast and outlet in humor. Such were the qualities by which the unknown writer held her readers. If further analyzed, the book shows experience, an eye for the deeper emotions and for the strange parody that plays havoc with our lives and brings results entirely opposite to those anticipated. It warns us by showing in a hollow mirror a contorted image of what is to be our lot. In this particular Fru Collett is certainly related to George Eliot. Margrethe gives Cold such good advice concerning the young girl who is to be his choice. "Do not ravish her love, let her feeling ripen of itself. Like the must, it needs time to ferment, and if it is pure, it will overflow of its own sweetness." But this restraining of his own emotion in order that hers may freely unfold, brings disaster. The story of the poor old spinster, once "the prettiest most fêted girl in all the parish," who went daft from shame because she had confessed her love to the man she loved, becomes to Sophie such a hollow mirror wherein she shudderingly sees her own fate parodied (for she did not go daft); while Cold's noble delicate remarks seem to her the flower-decked trap into which she falls.

This scene is with a great deal of art made the central point of the book. Here the chief actors show their characters, from here their fate is worked out in logical sequence. People's thoughts were especially occupied with the tendency of the novel. "What is it she wishes?" they said. "Does she want the ladies to propose?" Fru Collett herself says that she wished to reinstate feeling in its rights. She somewhere calls the book "a cry that escaped me, my life's long-withheld despairing cry." The book was indeed herself, what she had lived through, only resuscitated, risen from her soul's depth as another reality. Hence no one can criticize this work for shallowness, lack of inventive power, insufficiency of imaginative transformation. On the contrary, the poetic has become the real and the reality is absorbed in the poetic.

Why did this book come to be, in a sense, Fru Collett's only great creative contribution to our literature? She herself says she was not fond of writing, and found no satisfaction in forced productivity. Besides, a contempt for fiction, which sometimes develops with maturer years, seems to have taken possession of her. She says somewhere, "If those who truly had lived, even though the life had not been remarkable, would with the courage of truth tell their experience, people would have reading more effectual in the progress of mankind than many of the fables with which we are now punished."

In accordance with this view, she published her personal and family memoirs in *The Long Nights*. This book is one of the most interesting memoirs to be found in any literature, and is written not only with intensity of feeling but with evident enjoyment as well. Yet it seems to have brought its author at the time only unpleasant remarks;—"It is, of course, nothing but lamentations," she "speaks all the time herself," and more of that kind. Hence she nearly lost courage and desire to bring forth anything for a public so plainly unappreciative. "Ask the plant which never sees sunshine why it does not have flower after flower," she says in *Last Leaflets*.

But a great talent cannot be so easily crushed. It made a new opening for itself in which the unpleasantness of being exposed to the gaze of the public and the suffering it cost her to write disappeared before the enthusiasm of serving a cause, an idea. And the idea lay beforehand in her soul, as a seed ready for growth. "There are facts in our existence that are not worth thinking too deeply about," says Louise in *The Daughters*, "perhaps it is fortunate that so few do think about them. We, who are the equals of men in the scale of living beings, who are just as noble, just as gifted as they, and are unsullied by their vices, we; while we are the objects of their choice and refusal are yet valued so singularly low." On the whole, Louise, her fate, her speech, the entire episode relating to her in its bold bitter beauty, its terseness and energy, its harsh reality (it frightened people so that in the next edition Fru Collett had to tone it down a bit)—this entire portion of the book was already a challenge to a fight for the cause of woman.

Life had prepared Fru Collett for such a fight. She had herself experienced how unfortunate it is in youth to have only one's heart to live on because one's hands are tied. She had seen great talents among those of her own age "vegetate within the family and die the natural death so likely to come to gifts in a woman." And she looked further and saw that "our country cannot employ its daughters. A thousand forces are left unused, miserably wasted, as is the champignon, which the peasant not knowing its value or use tramples under foot." She had observed long before the gap between men's and women's morals, for almost every household in the parishes had its Borgia, its Bluebeard in miniature; and she had seen the honorable wives— the pale, mute, griefworn, degraded wives—of these scandalous husbands. And even more deeply impressed upon her was the fact that she had seen good natural abilities in women restrained till they were transformed into evil. She had herself lived through "the greatest sorrow a human being can undergo, and to the grief and bereavement was added the experience of *a widow's lot in this land*." For again she looked further and saw that for other widows it was no different; that a woman was nothing in herself, did not exist as an individual, as a member of society, but only as a member of a family. To free the individual, to set in motion the forces for good, became thus Fru Collett's aim. "Emancipation, this watchword of your scorn," she exclaims, "means nothing but the deliverance of women's good natural salutary gifts; it is the false womanliness in them that emancipation will do away with and will put the true womanliness in its place." Healthy activity in some practical or intellectual direction she declared would bring an important liberation. And such liberation "will react upon women's emotional life, making it healthier and stronger. The age of unhealthy overwrought sentiment will then be past."

Fru Collett in 1860

The necessity for the same moral duty, the same responsibility for man as for woman, was to her a matter of chief importance. And she who was herself so chaste that she had to battle with her own sensitiveness in order to touch moral questions, gave Mrs. Butler's *Voice in the Desert* a warm and deeply felt welcome. She took up these needed reforms in legislation as well as in literature. Her polemical *Woman in Literature* tore big rents in the accepted standards. Especially the French legislation and the French novel received the sharp arrows of her wit and her indignation. But also in our own literature she pointed out the painful fact that the type of woman had deteriorated.

Fru Collett now always wrote under her own name. The dual sides of her nature, which she recognized by having "Hardie et Timide" engraved in her seal, were no longer at war. She was timid for herself, but bold for her cause. The blows and adversity resulting from her battle she considered as afflictions undergone for the sake of her cause.

But she had not only adversity. She gained companions in arms as well, warm faithful friends and admirers. With bitter-sweet humor, she called herself a goodwife who tried to stem and turn the tide, and she named one of her books *Against the Tide*. Yet in time she found that the tide did turn her way, that her cause made progress. Her joy at this, at the opening of any new field to women, at every deed accomplished, every recognition gained, was touching and never to be

[99]

forgotten by those whom she gave approval and sympathy.

After her sons had grown to man's estate and a more than common stature, Fru Collett traveled a great deal and for the last thirty years of her life had no established residence at home. Her work drew her away, the chilly atmosphere drove her away. The soothing quality of Rome, the enlivening quality of Paris, the pleasure of living among artists, in the easier, freer life outside, had their attractions even for her. In later years, Copenhagen, so refreshing to Norwegians, became to her a second home. There she most often spent the winter. But longing for her family, homesickness for the beautiful land, the hard mother Norway, impelled her return. And thus she continued to live until even from the hard mother she received the great recognition. Her long often gloomy day passed away in a beautiful evening glow. A great multitude from all over the land paid homage to her on her eightieth birthday, bringing from each and every one a special expression of gratitude for the way she had awakened, spurred, strengthened, or simply given joy. Her reform work and her poetic work gathered into one great light which shone over the whole land. And a few years after, she died, at home, among her own, as she had desired.

Fru Collett's importance in the recent history of our country is great. Her unusual personality, possessing something of the fairy princess, something of the saga woman; her unique position in the centre of clashing views, with family relations and affections ranged against intellectual sympathies and educational affinities; her style, so elastic, graceful, strong and buoyant; her subjects and her treatment of them so superior that our knowledge of the country and the times would be incomplete without her writings; her battle as pathbreaker and pioneer for her sex;—all these secure to her an eminent rank among our remarkable personalities and our greatest authors.

"Like the diamond, she will preserve her lustre and her value."

NOTE ON WELHAVEN AND THE
FOLK POETRY

*(Translated by A. M. W. from Jaeger's History
of Norse Literature)*

ELHAVEN'S hope had been fulfilled, peace had settled upon the country, a quiet time had begun, a time when clearness and harmony could be enjoyed. The strife of the thirties no longer roused emotions either in politics or in literature. The law of self-government within the communes had been put into operation, the dissatisfaction with the union had subsided after the nation had obtained its own flag, and the stubborn Carl Johan had been succeeded by the accommodating Oscar the First. For the present the national excitement had gone down like water in a kettle taken off the fire. Even in literature there was peace and happiness. The real disturber of harmony (Henrik Wergeland) had retired and soon was to leave the field forever.

During these peaceful years a new element of literary life was discovered, which produced a movement short in time but great in importance. It was the existence of a "national" or folk poetry, a poetry preserved by the people itself as its own product and special property. Poets previously known were children of officials, brought up on the ideas of the period of enlightenment. What they had heard of the myths and tales belonging to the people had never gone beyond the nursery or the servants' hall. The enlightened parents regarded these things with true eighteenth century indifference;—they were but expressions of superstition, ignorance, and lack of taste which an enlightened person ought to disregard or even destroy. Their children, therefore, never learned to know the folk-myths thoroughly; and when as adults they became enthusiastic over them, because romanticism took such interest in national poetry and national life in general, they had no true conception of the treasures hidden away in the memories of the country population. When Fredrika Bremer in 1840 wrote to Henrik Wergeland requesting material for a description of Norwegian life in town and in country, he said among other things that he knew nothing of any national poetry or folklore. He supposed that such things existed, but he did not know definitely.

The interest in folklore and the belief in its importance for that poetry which is art had begun in Europe several generations before. Even as early as 1765 the Englishman Percy had published his "Reliques," which made an epoch; particularly in Germany, where Herder was led to a comprehensive study of the folklore of all countries and Bürger and Goethe used the folksong in their own poetry. Then came the romanticists and carried the matter further. All old German songs and tales were most carefully collected and the romantic poets produced both tales and songs of their own invention. In Denmark this new movement became important with Oehlenschlager. He worked over old Danish ballads and wrote original new ones; fairy tales and sagas he used for poetical reproduction, and Scandinavian mythology became a gold mine to him.

Norwegian poets whose ideas of poetry had been influenced by this new departure were really in a difficult and hopeless situation. Those subjects to which they would have most naturally turned, had already been used by Oehlenschlager, and in their opinion with such superior results that nothing was left for them to do. The sagas and the old mythology were lost to them, nothing remained but the songs and the tales. From them the revival of poetry had to come. (To these writers the poetry of Henrik Wergeland had no value— it was not "national.")

First of all it was necessary that the folksongs and stories be collected, and then that a poet appear who should know how to use them. Fortunately men were found who did the collecting—Asbjörnsen, Moe, and Landstad; and the poet supposed to have made the right fructifying use of the spirit embodied in this truly national poetry was Welhaven. Asbjörnsen and Moe were peasant boys, well acquainted from childhood with folklore and possessing a way of handling people that put the bashful narrator at ease. Their field was the collecting of fairy tales and myths. In 1842 they published their first volume. Landstad's work was the gathering of folksongs, particularly old ballads, and in 1853 he published a hundred of them. These volumes as a truly national heirloom were received with great enthusiasm. It was as if the Norwegian nature and the national poetry had suddenly been for the first time seen to exist. Like busy bees collectors and investigators swarmed all over the fields where something might yet be found. The musician Lindeman collected national songs as sung by the people. The Norse national costumes were pictured and described, the old Norse frame architecture was studied, and a society was formed to save what national monuments had not yet been destroyed. The history of Norway was also a subject of fruitful study; and the language as it appeared in the old sagas and in the dialects. Even the artists began to paint Norse scenery or historical events and picturesque groups of mountaineers in the old houses.

Finally the poets were taken by the same enthusiasm. The most important and most interesting literary figure of the period was without comparison Welhaven. Wergeland had worked for national education. Welhaven now became equally active for a new national poetry. Although Welhaven was not the creator of the new movement, he joined it so heartily that in his special field—lyric verse—he became the first and foremost, the one whose production determined and fructified the work of other poets. This is the more remarkable, since Welhaven had been an established writer with his individual character before the "national" movement began at all. Nevertheless, his participation in this movement became the central force in his poetry. What had preceded was but an introduction;

what followed was but a few harmonious closing chords. During his quarrel with Wergeland, Welhaven's thought and feeling had developed considerably. The poet had begun to unfold like a butterfly in its cocoon. But the final metamorphosis had not come then. He did not see the subject that truly inspired him till he found these national themes,—things sympathetically related to his innermost nature.

Indeed, Welhaven's peculiarly sensitive organism felt with special force the appeal of this folk-poetry. Hidden away like his own personal feeling, this poetry had lived in the innermost heart of the people, and hovered as an unknown uncomprehended spirit over the Norwegian nature, with its strange mingling of the enchanting and the stern. Even as early as 1840 Welhaven confessed to having been affected by this national spirit. It seemed to call to him "as a perennial alluring entreaty from mountain and forest; on every wooded slope he heard the suggestion of most touching immortal melodies—the spirits of the woods and fields stormed in upon him with a thousand memories and lamentations." Norway, as material for poetry, was indeed like a primeval forest where no man's foot had yet stepped and through which the Spirit of the North whisperingly wandered. With exultant joy Welhaven saw this new world opened to him and lost no time in taking possession of it. But not only was the national poetry discovered,—the Norwegian nature too was appreciated; its beauty, its majesty, its unspeakable virgin charm, and its defiant boldness. And Welhaven was the first to characterize

in poetry the far-stretching deep forests, the narrow
valleys surrounded by high peaks, and the tremendous
wildness and loneliness of the highlands. Nobody
expressed better than he did the secret charm of evening
twilight near the wooded shore of a mountain stream,
or described the calm coolness of a spruce forest on a
hot summer day; no one painted more exquisitely the
enrapturing beauty of a winter landscape, or the mystical loneliness of the deep forest.

But there is one side of his poetry which is particularly characteristic of the period and which separates
it from productions of previous and later times; that
is its relation to the folklore, or rather the folk-super-
stition. To Welhaven the huldre (woodnymph), the
elves, the nøk (watersprite) were personifications of
the moods that nature called forth—personifications
he used very often, and yet which for him were artificial
and acquired, not beliefs inherent and innate, as with
the people itself. Thus behind all was a lack of vitality
that impaired the truthfulness of his poetry—a vestige
of a literary fad that interfered with the lasting beauty
of the relation between nature and his own moods.
Nature seems to have been not sufficiently poetical in
herself, his æsthetic demands could not be satisfied with
things as they were; he would perfect them still more,
make nature still more beautiful by those reminiscences
of a past age. He intended in the huldre, the elves, and
the nøk to give the very essence of nature in plastic
representations; but he was not able to make them real
to the cultured sophisticated minds for which he wrote.

Welhaven himself did not believe in the huldre. She was to him an expression, not a feeling; and therefore she remained in his poetry a dead sign, interfering with genuine poetic impressiveness. In spite of the strong correspondence between the beauty of natural scenery and Welhaven's inner self, as soon as he began to handle this machinery of superhuman beings he lost his true bearing; he felt out of keeping with the fantastic element introduced and his lyric became cold and impersonal.

Besides these poems of nature, however, Welhaven wrote ballads treating of national events or local events of national interest, and these are his most perfect works of art. He never became very Norwegian in his language, but the spirit is Norse, if not the words; and therefore, he is after all, a national poet and will maintain his supremacy in his own somewhat limited sphere.

THE PROGRESS OF THE WOMAN MOVEMENT
IN NORWAY

ARY WOLLSTONECRAFT traveled through Norway in 1796 and said of the people: "The Norwegians appear to me sensible and shrewd, with little scientific knowledge and still less taste for literature, but they are arriving at the epoch which precedes the development of the arts and sciences. Most of the towns are seaports, and seaports are not favorable to improvement. By travel the captains acquire a little superficial knowledge which their fixed attention to the making of money prevents their digesting; and the fortune they thus laboriously gain is spent, as everywhere in towns of this description, in show and good living. They love their country but have not much public spirit. Their exertions are in general only for their families; which I conceive will always be the case till politics, becoming a subject of discussion, enlarges the heart by opening the understanding. The French Revolution will have this effect. At present they sing with great glee many republican songs and seem earnestly to wish that the republic may stand; yet they appear very much attached to their prince royal." Half a generation after Mary Wollstonecraft's visit came the downfall of Napoleon, the separation of Norway from Denmark, the Norwegian declaration of independence, and the constitutional convention followed by the personal

union with Sweden; a union which Sweden constantly but unsuccessfully tried to make a union in fact. Hand in hand with the persistent struggle for the maintenance of national integrity went the struggle for the upbuilding of the country and the elevation of the people, in order that Norway should worthily take its place among the freedom-loving and truly independent countries of the civilized world. The prophet who pointed the way and guided the steps toward this great goal and vitalized in his speeches and writings the spirit which had dictated the constitution was Henrik Wergeland.

The foregoing is the background of facts on which the woman movement in Norway must be pictured if it is to be understood in relation to the national life. The prophet and leader in that movement was the sister of Henrik Wergeland, Fru Camilla Collett. She became the first great national pioneer in a world movement of which the present generations are reaping the benefit. During the long weary years of her widowhood, Fru Collett reflected sufficiently upon the lot of women to see how false, unnatural and degraded was their position in the social whole; and from the fullness of her experience she proceeded to show the facts in novels and essays. There were others a little later than she, more radical, such as Aasta Hansteen, philosopher and propagandist, who sought the reason for the contempt of woman in the century-old religious prejudice against woman as an inferior being, not created in the image of God, but merely in the image of man and hence kept in subjection by him. Life was made as uncomfortable for Aasta Hansteen as for Fru Collett, and she came to the United States, to Boston, where she stayed six years. During her absence, however, reflection had come to her aid at home, and when she returned about 1892 she was received with appreciation. She afterward remained in Christiania witnessing the good seed bearing fruit.

About 1875 the women of the capital began to organize. The first indication of this was the formation of a Woman's Reading Club, to which Fru Collett and other prominent women were invited and which speedily accumulated a large library including papers and periodicals. It is now one of the noteworthy sights of the capital. Some years later was formed the Woman's Cause Association which gradually grew to enormous dimensions and to have affiliations all over the country. It has long been a power to be reckoned with both in social and political life. It was followed in 1885 by a Woman's Suffrage Association, the founder of which was Gina Krog. Two years later Gina Krog established a special organ for women's interests called *New Land*. In this periodical, then monthly, now semi-monthly, questions of importance for the welfare of women are discussed with great ability. This little paper has from the first worked great changes in public opinion. One of its best deeds has been the connection it established with phases of the movement in other countries. Its editor was later president of the National Council of Women and a member of the International Council of Women, a world-wide organization which exercises a great and well-merited influence even upon national legislatures. She has repeatedly been a delegate to the World's Congresses of Women held at Washington, Berlin, Copenhagen and other places. *New Land* has been the medium through which all movements relative to women's work and position have been presented,— the woman's peace movement, the prohibition movement, the white slave trade, and other problems more or less international as well as national and local.

In the fifties of the nineteenth century women were admitted to positions as telegraph operators and later to the postal service and telephone service, all of which are under state control. As teachers they have been busy, at first in small private schools for girls but afterwards also in larger private schools for boys. From the first both women and men have taught in the public schools, women having charge especially of the separate classes for girls. Their ability as teachers has always been recognized. The great question was equal wages for equal work. The advancement of women to positions of government in the schools and to equally prominent positions in the other branches of public service made the question vital. A petition was brought to the postal department from women clerks in the postoffices of the larger cities for increase of salary on an equal basis with men. It stated that the women did exactly the same work as the men, from the heaviest, such as handling mailbags, to the lightest; and that in the case of women who took care of registered mail, postal orders and other valuable possessions of the service, more than two hundred thousand crowns a day passed through their hands. Hence their responsibilities were fully as great as those of the men. This question *New Land* most ably advocated, and finally in 1908 equal reward for equal labor was conceded.

The heaviest battle, however, was fought over questions even more far-reaching—the participation of women in the government of commune and state. Woman's communal suffrage was granted as far back as 1883 but was vetoed by the king. In 1893 it almost passed the house. In 1901, however, communal suffrage was given to tax-paying women, married or unmarried; i. e., they were given the right to sit in the communal council, apportion taxes, look after the support for schools, the poor, the roads, and such matters. This victory merely whetted the appetite for other and better things. That very year forty-eight thousand four hundred and two women voted, ninety-eight women were elected as members and a hundred and sixty as deputies. Four years later, in 1905, events took place which concerned women no less than men. The separation from Sweden occurred, which might have stirred up a most bitter and bloody war, had not international complications prevented it and calmed the irate Swedish crown prince. When the tension was at its highest the ministry made an appeal to the nation (not merely to a party) for support in its policy; and the women, who considered themselves as much concerned as the men, demanded to be given a voice in the plebiscite called for by the ministry in regard to the separation from the Swedish alliance and the selection of a Norwegian king. The ministry in its announcement of the result paid no attention to the women's demand but referred only to the men. Great dissatisfaction was felt, indignation meetings were held and petitions circulated. Finally an address was presented to the president of the Storting with three hundred thousand signatures, practically of all grown Norwegian women, expressing their unanimous support of the action of the ministry. The president of the Storting received the address with grateful recognition, and when he read it from the presidential chair all members rose from their seats. It would have been interesting could Fru Collett have been there that day. But Aasta Hansteen was. Evidently the ministry felt that it had most unwisely snubbed the women and jeopardized public opinion at a critical moment, for when the Storting assembled in 1906 two bills for women's suffrage were considered, one for limited suffrage, that is, for all women over twenty-five who paid tax on a certain amount of property; and the other for unlimited—suffrage on the same basis as men's. The agitation was substantially helped by the fact that women of Finland at that time were given full franchise. Finland had hitherto followed Norway in all matters of politics. The Norwegian Storting could not be less generous than the Finnish diet. In great suspense the outcome was awaited, and on June 13, 1907, the limited suffrage bill passed the house. Some three hundred thousand were benefited by it.

New Land, however, did not let it rest there. Complete franchise was the cry! In 1910 the law was passed granting to women general communal suffrage, and at last in 1913 by a unanimous vote of the Storting women were given entirely unrestricted franchise.

The most important leader in these final achievements was Fru Qvam. In an article on politicians in Norway Wilhelm Keilhan writes about Fru Qvam: "She can look back upon more victories and fewer defeats than almost any of her contemporaries among the men. It was in 1898 that she appeared as a leader in the woman movement. To be sure, the movement had claimed an existence for a decade but it had gained no definite results. Its organization had not extended beyond a narrow circle of women in the metropolis and it had not been able to wield any noticeable influence on public opinion. But in a comparatively few years the new aggressive movement which Fru Qvam organized together with Gina Krog, Hedvig Rosing, Aasta Hansteen and other well-known women had spread throughout the land. In quite a remarkable way the movement under Fru Qvam's direction succeeded in evading its most dangerous enemy—ridicule and laughter. Possessed of unusual reticence and rare tact, she became a master as a lobbyist. During her active career she was called "the little queen of the corridors." Though the other women mentioned gave invaluable aid, Fru Qvam made the movement great, and by her wonderful strategic powers won success after success till full suffrage was attained. She is universally recognized as one of the greatest politicians, in a good sense, that Norway has ever had."*

Of course, there have come into existence other phases of women's activity besides the political. It is worth noting that in 1882 the national university was opened to women students as well as to men and the same year the first woman was matriculated. From a still earlier date women had been doing individual investigative work under the auspices of the university and now there are women with rank and title in the university who do that kind of work and publish their papers in the university proceedings.

Of women in professional life there are many. Two women attorneys are pleading in the Supreme Court. In 1910 two women were appointed by law as factory inspectors. Female police exist for the protection of children and young people in public places. Numerous practising physicians and dentists are women. We have one woman steamship agent who is held in great repute, and any number of tradeswomen—bookbinders, watchmakers, and others. There has been much agitation for maintaining married women in public service. A woman's sanitary union is actively combating consumption and other white plagues and maintaining hospitals for unmarried mothers and invalids. Last but not least, legalized prostitution is a thing of the past for the whole land.

*It may be of interest to recall the fact that on June 5, 1915, equal suffrage became legal in Denmark.—ED.

Henrik Ibsen

IBSEN AND THE NORWEGIANS

ANY of those indebted to Ibsen for his inspiring works scarcely think to inquire about the temper of the nation and the character of the country from which he came. Even in this day of travel, little occurs to some minds when Norway is mentioned but the trite phrase "land of the midnight sun." Yet that is an exceedingly misleading expression. For except in the far north, Norway has summer and winter, day and night, very much like the rest of the world. Besides this general indifference and ignorance, the severity of Ibsen's attacks on Norse society has undoubtedly caused some misunderstanding of both the author and the country. The sources of this severity have not, I believe, been fully seen by foreign critics. Some have ascribed it to his lack of sympathy with the home land, to an alienation almost instinctive and due to his mixed blood. German critics especially have reiterated that he had half a dozen nationalities in his make-up. No wonder, they say, that he possessed such versatility, such cosmopolitan breadth of view, such tendency toward speculation, and such puritanism in his demands on his fellow-men. He got them all from his German and Scotch ancestry. But this reasoning appears rather strained. For many others, purely Norwegian in blood, have also been alienated from their country. Besides, an intellect of the highest order must

[117]

always be cosmopolitan. Even Henrik Wergeland, staunchest of patriots, felt that he belonged not to Norway alone but to the whole world.

As a matter of fact, Ibsen was to the core a good patriot. Mixed blood did not prevent this. Norse history shows that a complex ancestry and foreign extraction never produced traitors to the national feeling. Large numbers of our merchant and even of our official classes are of Dutch-German or Dutch-English descent. Englishmen and Frenchmen frequently marry into Norwegian families, or Norwegians take German or English wives, and the generation that follows is usually more patriotic than even the pure-blooded native. No one shouts more lustily and praises more lovingly the virtues of the Modern Norway than they. Ibsen's patriotism, however, was not like theirs. I think he held the name of country still more sacred, and from pride or natural delicacy spoke least of what he loved most. During all the years of "exile," as he called it, he never lost sight of events at home. He watched them with the utmost attention and solicitude. If he were so alienated as some would have us think, why did he not abandon us altogether, become a citizen of many lands, and write in a foreign tongue? Instead, he remained the faithful son of a small country, and life in that country was the one subject on which he wrote. Who can blame him if he wished, like the rest of us, to enlarge the mental horizon of his native land, and see it expand in will and purpose? All of our poets have had this wish—Björnson perhaps less than others. Björnson* thought Norway was pretty good as she was, and thus he became the leader of the ultra patriots. Ibsen, on the other hand, in his strong revulsion against all that smacked of self-righteousness and absolutism, used the probing knife rather than the velvet glove. No doubt he spoke from the housetops what some of us had courage only to whisper to ourselves; and although it is a fearful trial to have the cat-o'-nine-tails applied to one's quivering flesh, and still more fearful to have this done with every one looking on in amazement and scorn, though too he seemed sometimes to cut dangerously near the seat of life, yet we feel now that we were too apprehensive. We see that he freed us from the greatest of all evils—lethargy; and that in the big problems before us of building the state anew, his stern hand pointed out the readiest solution.

As for his notable tendency toward speculation, this is as essentially Norwegian as it is German. It was merely increased by the philosophic training that a thoughtful reader and independent thinker like Ibsen inevitably receives from contact with the world at large.

If then, though cosmopolitan in experience and interest, Ibsen yet remained truly Norwegian in his patriotic spirit and his philosophic habit, one expects to find some other explanation than foreign ancestry for his so-called puritanical sternness. The real explanation for that unmitigated severity, which as Gosse

*See Appendix II on Björnson.

[119]

somewhere says "borders on the tyrannical," is found, I am convinced, in the nature of the country where he was born and where his youth and early manhood were spent. Impressions received then are never quite effaced in anybody; and it is not too much to say that Norway is one of the most impressive, least forgetable of countries. Ibsen's unflinching idealism expresses the very essence of its character.

One who has stood on those mountain heights and looked out over miles and miles of more mountains, top upon top, lying in the marvelous coloring of those regions and disappearing in the far distance, finds created in his breast an inexpressible longing, a yearning and pining for still loftier heights, for an ideal that seems at once near and very far away. It beckons and urges him to approach, to brave fatigue and hardship to reach it, to bathe his soul in its glorious revelation—and he alone can fully measure the quality of the burning eagerness and determination that animate Ibsen's writings. For Norwegians he was the guide who pointed out and led to these heights of thought, these vast spaces away from the sultry sordid life below. From those heights the poet's voice reached us like a clarion call in his first long poems, and in his last he seems to take leave of everything and disappear in their mists.

The superior view of life granted from the heights is not, alas, what one gets in the valley beneath. The valleys of Norway are not open dales with smiling villages and beautiful, spreading, dark-leaved trees, as in Switzerland. Instead, there are the fir, the juniper, and the white-stemmed birch, all slender, courting the sunshine, enduring of temper, battling incessantly for more room. These clothe the bleak sides of the rock with their dark and light hued foliage. Besides, there are moss and heather, beautiful fine grasses and tiny flowers. Such is the vegetation of the Norwegian valleys—indicative of a meager soil sparsely distributed and only gradually wrested from the towering mass of granite above. This is particularly true near the West coast where the narrowness of the valleys become exaggerated. Here the mountains rise almost perpendicularly from the sea, and the sea penetrates far into the very heart of the mountains until but a tiny strip of shore is left on either side of the fjord. There cling little groups of buildings, fishing villages that can scarcely be called even villages, and trading places crouching in the very shadow of the snowclad mountain overhead. In these valleys and on the clusters of islets and ledges which break the terrible onset of water and wind, lives a considerable part of our population, perhaps the most courageous and gifted part of it. No wonder that under the pressure of the severest daily toil these people have thought of the mountains as their prison wall and have sought success and fortune always beyond. The sea with its unlimited possibilities has proved the salvation of the Norse people, and it is chiefly due to the enterprise and hardihood of our coast population that Norway ranks fourth in the world's commerce. Fancy what this means to a country of only two and a half million people! No wonder the Norse sailor figures everywhere, in the English navy and in the commercial fleet of every nation. But when thrust back on themselves, the people that live in these narrow valleys find little to feed their energy and often eat their hearts out in restlessness or mute despair.

If Ibsen did not fall into or remain in such states of mind, he shows abundantly that he understood them. His active critical idealism compelled him to be up and out, to pass into the wider ranges of thought; and it forced him at the same time to try to take his countrymen with him to nobler planes of living. But his efforts were not then understood. This lack of understanding brought about his self-imposed exile. In his *Emperor and Gallilean* there is a remark that may be singularly well applied to himself. Julian says of Libianus that he was a great man because he had suffered a great wrong and was filled with a noble wrath. The word "noble" here is all important. Did Ibsen think of his own case when he wrote this? We shall never know. What we do know is that he felt he had been done a grievous wrong by the people whom he had served when the coldness of some and the abusive criticism of others literally drove him out of the country and compelled him for seventeen years to live and compose in foreign lands. *Brand, Peer Gynt, The League of Youth, Emperor and Galilean,* were sent home after his departure and the Storting granted him a lifelong stipend to encourage him further. But the conservative faction among the newspapers continued to set up a howl of derision every time a new work appeared, and he felt himself bereft of the right kind of appreciation at home even after he had begun to make for himself a European reputation. The wrath with which he was filled he determined to turn to account, not only to shame those who presumed to be his judges but to remove from the nation that conceit which is a sure mark of ignorance, so that others following his calling should not in future suffer as he had.

We all know how he set about his task, and his self-imposed mission certainly resulted in an altered attitude toward our authors and poets, even the most radical. After the storm had subsided which followed the publication of *The League of Youth*, in which he satirizes the tendencies of Norwegian local politics, he was for a time silent except for the letter he sent home in 1872 on the millenial celebration of the existence of Norway as a united kingdom. In this, after a brief prelude in which he greets his people from afar and reminds them of his exile and of the bitterness of solitude in strange lands, he begs them to fight a second time the battle of Hafrsfjord, not as of old with ships and soldiers but with ideas, to liberate the nation from the spirit of intolerance and persecution and to effect an inner higher union such as it had not hitherto known. I remember well the appearance of this fervent appeal—an appeal which was also a warning. He spoke less as a man to his fellows than as a king addressing his subjects or a prophet his

[123]

erring brethren. The stanzas rolled with a pathos like the tones of a pipe-organ. Little as I then understood it all, I can still feel the shiver of premonition and awe which passed through me, the profound sorrow for ourselves and for the poet. Seldom has a nation received so imperious a call from one whom it accused of indifference to its best interests.

His appeal, however, met very little response just then. We had closed our hearts to Ibsen at that time. We thought it strange that we should be criticized so much. Norway, we argued, was certainly no backwoods country. It was to all appearance in the front rank of both material and intellectual progress. Our painters, our composers, our authors, among them Ibsen himself, were no longer merely local celebrities. And we calmly assumed the correctness of Fischer's dictum: "Der welcher schumpft hat meistens unrecht." Ibsen, however, saw that the political disagreement of that time began to deteriorate into a mere squabble, that the disturbances consumed our strength; and his soul waxed too bitter within him to mince words. In this respect Björnson was entirely different. He always enjoyed a fight. In his books there is always some one fisticuffing some one else. But to Ibsen's more patrician taste the noise and the abuse which political strife always brings seemed highly repellent. Much, of course, could be said to justify or condemn this incident in the national life. One thing is sure, a small country must be alive, every atom of it, if it is to maintain itself in the battle for room and power among the

[124]

nations, and political commotion is generally the most
direct way of keeping every one stirred and wide awake.

Ibsen, however, demanded freedom from within as
the only real guarantee for the perfect political freedom we coveted; and no one can say he was not right.
To clean the atmosphere of its putrid elements, this
alone could keep us in health; to turn to introspection, to reveal and combat our weaknesses, this alone
could make us strong and above all, true. And thus
he began his crusade against social prejudice and
injustice.

These distinctly national conditions, then, are the
real sources of that uncompromising severity which
some have named puritanical. It was too deeply
ingrained and sprang from too profound suffering, both
actual and imaginative, to have been produced merely
by mixture of foreign blood, by an exaggerated cos-
mopolitanism, or by personal resentment. Most intense
nationalism, living faith in his country, and in mankind, was its primitive origin. Unfaith and pessi-
mism were only the superficial appearances which his
rebukes to his people assumed in the eyes of those less
clear-sighted.

Two great works of Ibsen are so profoundly national
in their source, in their appeal, and in their revelation of character, that perhaps only a native can
entirely comprehend them. Though given to the world
at large, *Brand* and *Peer Gynt* present Norwegian
types and preëminently belong to Norwegians.

[125]

Mention has been made of the repressing effect which the uncompromising mountains have on the dwellers in the narrow coast valleys. That abnormal repression must needs find an outlet. From among this coast population, crushed at times into apparent muteness, more than elsewhere in Norway, arise ultraists and fanatics who carry their demands and their speculations far beyond what the church and the state permit. God appears to them as a terrible lord of sufficiency whom no prayer or supplication can move. The stagnation of the Lutheran Church has been broken from time to time by preachers who have generally hailed from these districts and who have traversed the country convulsing congregations with tears and moanings for their sins. Of course a persecution soon followed such offenders, yet a shock had been felt. Even within the Church itself the spirit of contradiction and criticism has now and again awakened. In my childhood I often passed the house where one of the arch offenders spent his last years, shunned and forgotten, a lonely, struggling, sad man; but for all that, to the Church he had defied, he had been a harbinger of freer spirit and truer life. Ibsen's *Brand* presents such a preacher, such a militant soul who rests not satisfied with what is transmitted but tries to reach greater depths, nobler heights, and perishes in the conflict.

The book is a combination of various elements of revolt against the Church as a state institution. It dates from the period of the great pietistic movement in Norway, and is in the widest sense a poetical philosophical summary of the interest for life of such a wave of strong religious feeling and fanaticism as that period witnessed. This great matter certainly touched Ibsen's searching mind more than any other man's, far or near. It is with the glaring light of his Diogenes lantern that he reveals a story of fierce domination and unintelligent submission, followed by as fierce a popular revolt and the inward conviction of failure. If any moral sentence were to be chosen as the motto of the book, it might be that of Goethe: "Licht, mehr Licht!" Ibsen is questioning the right and value of the spiritual supremacy that some ardent natures claim (in religious matters) over their fellow-beings, and he shows the form such spiritual supremacy takes when the mind is powerfully agitated.

Historically, the first rebel against the Church was the Danish philosopher Kirkegaard, who was himself a theologian and minister. Kirkegaard's attacks on the Church as a state institution were severe in the extreme. He made the whole thing crumble under his blows. He declared that he would rather commit the worst crime than set his foot in a church. He was of course bitterly assaulted by the Press—not the least so because he like Ibsen considered it his chief business to ask questions rather than to answer them. The other noted representative of conscious revolt within the Church was Pastor Lammers, pastor in Skien, Ibsen's native town. He had been pastor for twenty years when he declared that he could stand it no longer and resigned. In his last sermon he called the churches houses of comedy and the official divine service idolatry; and he refused to be a hypocrite any longer, even for dear daily bread. He founded a free congregation which later met in the open air, the church proving too small.

The mind of Brand is that of a critic. His exasperation gets the better of him and he strikes out right and left. He is unproductive, but he at least tries to clear the road of debris. He is the type of a leader, a prophet, a spiritual fire, as his name indicates; a reformer who wishes to strike down and annihilate by the blaze of his wrath the dull vicious vermin that poison the world and infect the pastoral herd, and to put up instead, a new altar and establish a new devotion to God. He means to wake up people with his word as well as with his example. Full of unflinching belief in his right and his mission, he is a zealot with as narrow a view of Christianity as any of the fanatics fostered in those valleys where the mountains crowd out the sky and the hardships of life seem to lie in wait for one's very soul. Severe as is existence, are the views of all those that strive for it. The word "sin" covers such a vast field of harmless enjoyment! Minds there are shy and bitter, the deadening of the flesh is the highest achievement comprehended. The most innocent play incites severe proof;—how can feeling or compassion, warmth of heart and spontaneity, not freeze and crystalize in such surroundings?

Brand is as erring in his converting frenzy as are those that beguile him and finally drive him out beyond

the boundaries of his parish into the lonely wilderness
to perish in the cold and snow. This failure to find
any response, this absolute defeat of his mission,
strikes a harder blow than his exposure and his unhap-
piness. Doubt, feeling of inability to understand more
than one side of the reforming work, gnaws on his
conscience; he is overcome and in the anguish of death
the cry goes up to heaven whether after all he has not
been mistaken, whether the unswerving energy of his
man's will shall not be the quality that redeems him.
He receives as answer that God is not the God of law
but of love. Thus Brand sinks perishing at the feet
of the mercy he has not understood, and the snow-
storm that has swept around him covers him up and
extinguishes the last sparks of the fire that burned so
fervently.

The representatives of officialdom in the poem are
and are not true to nature. Of course all officials were
not unscrupulous nor heartless nor bootlicks, as are
the Dean and the Mayor. Yet there is a large kernel
of truth in the character of each as Ibsen gives it.
The civil official class, typified in the Mayor, was
inclined to view itself as the bearer of culture, insight,
wisdom and practical understanding; it played Providence to the common man, denying him sense or judgment. Whoever did not belong to that class was looked
down upon as inferior. This is even today a fault of
the official class, much as everywhere in Europe. The
feeling of superiority was especially evident with
regard to the peasants, who in matters of law were

often helpless in the hands of the officials. Henrik Wergeland died financially ruined partly because of the many lawsuits in which he engaged to defend peasants who appealed to him for help against the often unscrupulous officials. Of course all these servants of the law were patriots in their way, they strove as they thought sincerely for the welfare of the country, but they certainly did not get the sympathy or confidence of the people.

The Dean, as a representative of the clerical official class, is an even more vicious type. Suave, unctious, fearful of giving offense to the high, he stands for those in the upper ranks of churchmen who felt themselves first and foremost to be not shepherds but officials. The cant resorted to on festival days and heard likewise from the pulpit resounds even now in my ears. As often happens, they were high livers, yielding to none in fondness for rich eating and excellent wines, plus the jokes which are engendered by plentiful food. It is unnecessary to say that the Church which these men represented was to the people an object of indifference and even contempt. One reason for this was the activity shown by such clergy in persecuting the lay preachers, some of whom were true apostles of the faith. When the reaction came, this class of our priesthood was by popular vote excluded from representation in the Storting; whereas before they had been almost all-powerful. Thus ended their saga.

Though Ibsen may have had some sympathy with the particular phases of life shown in *Brand*, he had

none with those represented in *Peer Gynt*. In these,
his polemic inclinations found a fit subject for attack.
While our mountain valleys harbor the most gifted and
energetic portion of our population, as the rarest
most exquisite flowers grow under the very brow of the
snow, yet there are others, perhaps negligible as individuals though not as a class, in whom the divine dis-
content is not. Indifferent, shiftless, they are given to
bolstering themselves up with a false respectability
which, however, they are quick to throw away when
there is no palpable gain in keeping it. Such characters form the riff-raff of every country; the loudest
politically, pushing forward on every occasion, clam-
oring for themselves, wielding and wasting power
until the "still in the land" grow weary with the
tumult. This type Ibsen has immortalized as a national
mock-hero. Since the days of Aristophanes perhaps
no greater satire than *Peer Gynt* was ever written
on a people nor one in which every thrust leaves so
indelible a mark. Yet all is done without a tinge of
the abuse which disfigures the pamphleteering of the
Greek. Nor did anything Ibsen ever wrote strike
home to the dullest as did this. It showed another
side of the national character, the seamy side, too
often in evidence, alas, during the period from 1860
to 1890. The broader human quality of the poem
appeals to us more now than it did at the time of its
appearance, when it smote us hip and thigh. *Brand*
was at first beyond the ken of the majority; it was too
subtle, too combative, too acute in its suffering. But

Peer Gynt—the animated discourse, the bits from fairy tale and folklore, the dancing rhythm, the change of scenery, the jauntiness of the whole conceit, and withal the stinging quality of its wit, burning the tongue as one recited it—nothing equal to that was ever written among us. And it was at once comprehended. In fact, it has become the Norseman's Bible. He reads it, ponders it, quotes it, draws on every occasion from its inexhaustible drollery and sarcasm.

Although it has been translated with some success, it is untranslatable in its essence, in the spirit of that taunting rippling laughter which echoes through the whole. Those who read *Peer Gynt* in English will never quite fathom what an insufferable cad and bungler is this country lad who becomes a business man with the motto: business for business' sake; who turns into a globe-trotter; yet whose egotism serves only to make him sourly sceptical toward everything. And still he is determined that nobody and nothing shall change him. Thus he returns home, craftily evading the admonitions of conscience, and even escaping death, which waits for him on every crossroad and which would quite catch him were it not for an old white-haired woman, his former sweetheart, whom he had left a blooming girl. She is the only one who now welcomes him. Thus ends the poem; whether in seriousness or irony, who shall say? With me it has always left the impression of irony, yet Grieg's music refutes every thought of this. No wonder that foreigners find the poem, with its scenes shifting from

the Norwegian mountain peak to the desert Sahara,
with its many yarns, its allusions, hits and quips right
and left—no wonder that foreigners find it a most
baffling production, something midway between a farce
and a fantasy.

To foreigners the typical Norwegian often appears
the most stolid of beings. Ibsen, however, did not
choose his type at random. The type he portrays
is the peasant, but by no means the better kind
of peasant. The Norse peasant at his best is a
very aristocratic husbandman. He is neither a
fool nor a knave, neither obsequious nor lacking in
deference. His quiet but perfectly self-possessed bearing is usually characterized by the very best breeding.
He is at once modest, kindly, and firm. With a few
words he sets the stranger right who attempts to impose
on him. Foreigners detect this peculiar aloofness,
as does the native from the city who during vacation
mingles with the country people. An American traveller
declared she would as little have dared to address
a duchess uninvited as to address some of the plain
women she met on the highroad walking to church in
their national costume. There is something in their
manner which forbids familiarity. It was the peasant
woman, not the American, who pleasantly bade the
stranger good day.

Hence the appalling effect on a foreigner of such
revelations as those in *Peer Gynt*. Such a peasant as
this is to him a new type. But to us the poem is blood
of our blood, bone of our bone, and the fantastic ele-

ment makes it only so much the more bewitching to our inherent love of the extraordinary. For the Norseman loves satire; he is keenly alive to its sting, now deadly, now salutary, and never is satire more irresistible to his sense of the ludicrous than when it apparently flatters his folly and leads him unawares into admitting how utterly absurd and execrable such doings really are. As Ibsen became more Europeanized he lost this inimitable touch of raillery which drew a smile even while it drew blood, his blows fell heavier, the lashes seemed to leave scars on the body of the nation after the whipping was over. So at least some of us felt it. But the satire in *Peer Gynt* is lighter, more genial, and is even more unanswerable than the bitterer satire of the later social plays.

And yet even in the social plays the satire is too keen and clear-sighted to allow him to be dogmatic. As one translator says of him, "his most definite and dominant thoughts come to the surface laden with that tangle of counter-thought which gathers about every peremptory conclusion in the depths of a critical mind." It is well to remember these lines. Humanity has no heroes to Ibsen, unless it be some of his women. The figures are never seen with a naive admiring glance, but rather with a searching eye in order to bring out their whole character, to give the *sense* about them, if you will.

The social novel is usually the forerunner of the social drama. In France the best representative of the social novel in the first half of the century was undoubtedly George Sand, an author whose tremendous influence on fiction and drama alike is scarcely yet fully recognized. The first social novel in Norse or in any Scandinavian literature was Camilla Collett's *The Magistrate's Daughters.* This novel inaugurated in Scandinavia the movement for the liberation of women from the tutelage of centuries. That movement, since become a world issue, was then an extreme novelty except to those who had read George Sand or were familiar with the Comtean philosophy. John Stuart Mill's Essay on the Subjection of Women appeared in 1869, Fru Collett's novel in 1855; so that she was well ahead of him. Mill wrote from sympathy, Fru Collett from her own bitter experience. Throughout her life she kept the subject before the public in a succession of essays wherein she discussed in the wittiest way the prevailing type of woman in literature, in society, and in public estimation. Fru Collett and Ibsen were well acquainted; they met often during their periodic sojourns at Munich, Dresden, or Rome. Fru Collett could not abide the type of woman represented by Solveig in *Peer Gynt.* The namby-pamby femininity that endures and forgives with a sweetness which cloys on the reader was to her mind man's worst enemy. How could he have anything but contempt for that kind of nonentity? One is often confronted with this sort of woman in Ibsen's early dramas—the long-suffering Agnes, outraged by Brand in her most sacred affections; Solveig crooning over her returned lord when he deigns to observe her waiting arms; Dagny in the *Chieftains of Helgeland*, always whimpering and shocked; Fru Bernick, and a number of others undoubtedly portrayed from nature, are all of the same pattern and are too easily ignored by sovereign man. But in Ibsen's first social drama, *The Pillars of Society*, a new type not altogether unfamiliar but with a modern vital air not observed before, made its appearance. Among the perplexed womenkind of Consul Bernick's household, Lona Hessel is like a fresh breeze from the sea blowing from the world of decision and action. Lona sets things a-going, she inspires confidence in the hesitating, rescues the helpless, and makes Bernick, the arch hypocrite, acquire the semblance of a man. But she has been abroad, she is just back from the United States, and she almost compels by mere example the others to follow her when she returns.

Fru Collett always claimed that Lona Hessel was by suggestion her creation. Ibsen habitually pondered the criticisms he received. Fru Collett's ideas of womanly dignity evidently sank deeply into his mind. He had always been woman's just defender, and hitherto in his characterization he had been divided between the type of the saga woman, the heroic Norse woman proper, on the one hand; and on the other hand, a type more commonplace and mellow, but vastly inferior in strength. Now he brought forth the new woman, the woman of ideas, who refused to be an appendix, "an adjustable zero for the swelling of the sum total," as Fru Collett expressed it. With every new drama, as is now generally recognized, Ibsen devoted more

study to his women; and the action and effect of his
later plays are determined far more by them than by
the men. In the final words of the first social drama
he issued his dictum: Neither women nor men are the
"pillars of society," but Truth and Justice; and the
last act of *The Doll's House* expresses the revolutionary creed which he was to unfold and reassert in
work after work—Find thyself, be thyself!

Nevertheless, he did not stand so absolutely as some
critics have thought for individualism first and last.
That sounds a little too much like a celebration of
egotism, and to this Ibsen was vehemently opposed.
His demand was much more strictly ideal. He asked
for the true man, "the man as God saw him in His mind
on the day of creation," the man with character and
yet humble, the man that knows his own will and yet
is obedient, the man that has learned much, broadened
his spirit, and is full-grown in mind and body. Herein
is his point of contact with Goethe. But though
Goethe became serenely tranquil and synthetic in his
teaching, Ibsen remained to the last the born revolutionary and analyst.

Another contention of the critics deserves some
notice. Ibsen is sometimes classed with the authors
of poetic thought rather than with those of poetic
form, and he is denied beauty of form. And yet to all
Norwegians, yes, to all Scandinavians, Ibsen is the
master of form par excellence, none of our poets being,
as he is, the absolute artist that bends and shapes the
language into perfect rhyme and perfect rhythm alike.

Surely he is no Tennyson. He carries the sword rather than a wreath of roses; but his weapon is as finely wrought and well tempered as any masterpiece of Damascus. The Norse tongue with its stock of good dialect words, is capable, we are proud to say, of expressing whatever an artist may choose to confide to it; and Ibsen has been able not only to use it with virtuosity but also to increase even further its capacity of expression. The question, therefore, of his superiority of form may safely be left with his own people, who have long deemed him beyond criticism on that point.

"SECOND-SIGHT" IN NORSE LITERATURE

THE romantic movement in Europe in the late eighteenth century brought about a recognition in literature of what is peculiar, individual and original, and thus opened the way for character study—a most important form of realism. This character study, however, has with some recent writers lost almost all its realism and has become rather an exploration of the mystic depths of the human soul, particularly as these reveal themselves in anticipation of approaching bliss or doom. Strong contrasts are the means used, are perhaps the only means, of sounding these vague misty depths. Maeterlinck's plays were the first works that transplanted a reader from the life of day to the realm of shadows where thoughts and feelings yet unborn slowly take shape under his eyes, often in an icy cavelike atmosphere whither sun and life do not penetrate and only anticipation lives. Reality—flesh and blood—seem brutal here; the soul alone, or it is better to say only the trembling nerves, whisper through the twilight and the night.

In Norse literature, so far as I know, we have as yet nothing of this exaggerated form of mysterious soul revelation. Even Ibsen does not pretend to anything of that kind. His mysticism or symbolism reaches its climax in open deed, is after all transparent, does not flow out in anticipation merely. The vague floating-nowhere, the vibrating-about-what does not as yet appeal to the nation. It is not "decadent" in the full sense of the term. It covets the deed in preference to the dream. Introspection has an active rather than a passive character. And yet, to the close observer, Norse literature too, in folklore and popular belief, reveals an element similar to that mysterious somnambulic existence which an art-product of another literature has pictured for us. This peculiar element is the belief that certain people possess what is called "second-sight," or a sixth sense. Strange people they are, shut up to the outside visible world and ill at ease in it, but open to an invisible supernatural world. They are forced by unexplained and unavoidable compulsion to watch the inner mysterious motions and connections between the two worlds to which others are blind. Only through their unexpected and often terrifying consequences do most men become aware of these inexplicable mysteries.

The point that makes this supernatural element in Norse thought of peculiar interest is that it is general. It is not only a special motif handled with dexterity by an artist to create a great momentary impression upon more highly organized minds, but it is also a characteristic still active in the broad layers of the population. It is believed in and testified to by numerous tales and anecdotes that any one may hear who spends an evening in a friendly circle where ghost stories and strange events are related. This superstition has found a place among the masterpieces of our literature in a tale written some years ago by the justly famous Jonas Lie, and taken up again by him in later productions. Inasmuch as the story puts the case more clearly than any general reference to popular legends could do, it is here related in outline. In the original, its value is not only in its literary charm, in the marvelous beauty and power with which it is told, but quite as much in the unique incident itself. The chief figure is a man who possesses that sixth sense, that ability to receive warnings from those mysterious powers with which present-day spiritualism is particularly concerned.

When the story opens, this man has become a hermit, without much energy, seeking only a bare living, unable to bend under any yoke, needing the absolute liberty he claims. He knows he is abnormal, unfit for life, absorbed in memories, serving a painful almost horrible power that at intervals carries him out of himself and forces him to see as with eyes not his own what is hidden to all others. When these moments of strange compulsion come, he shuns every one, leaves everything behind, and wanders out into the forests and among the wide hills for days till the unrest has ceased and the attack is over.

He himself relates how this peculiar visionary malady has been shown in his life. When a child of seven years playing at his mother's feet, he suddenly in the open door sees a sweet sad-looking lady with a rose in her hand beckoning to him; and as he hesitates, she disappears. He tells his mother of the vision. She

at first sits transfixed in terror, then presses him to
her breast and bursts into tears. After that he sees
little of her, for she becomes hopelessly insane. His
father is a merchant, quiet, laborious, upright, with
nothing of this strange faculty, and suffering keenly
from the hopeless condition of his wife. For years
the son has no second visitation and has nearly forgotten about his peculiar faculty when on a night of
fearful gale, dreading the loss of fortune and life of
servants at sea, he suddenly sees as he stands in his
father's room the man about whom they are particularly anxious hanging dead in the rigging of the demolished ship. He swoons at the sight and is taken to bed.
But the news comes soon enough that the vessel has
gone on shore and everybody is lost.

He is then sent away and recovers perfectly; return-
ing only after he has become a young man with excellent health and fresh courage. At a ball he meets the
girl with whom he played while a child and for whom
he now feels another more consummate affection. She
returns his feeling and his life seems to open up brighter
than ever before. He has just stepped away after a
dance with her in the first crowning emotion of love
and is watching her dance with another, when the same
dreadful sense of impending calamity, of being forced
to see what he does not wish to see, comes over him.
The beautiful blooming girl, happy and full of life,
changes before his eyes into a pale dead one with sea-
grass clinging to her dress and water streaming from
her hair. He faints as before and has to be carried

out of the room. The next day the lovers meet and he tells her that he is not well, that dreadful images haunt him, that he can never be certain of freedom from them. And he proposes that they separate. But she will hear nothing of the kind; she declares that they have to bear this burden together and insists on her belief that their love will cure him. He allows himself to be persuaded. A week afterward, however, his beloved drowns while crossing the fjord, and when he sees her again it is exactly as he saw her that night while dancing. All hope of happiness is henceforth crushed. He lives on, bereft and in delicate health, wishing for death. His attacks become more frequent, but his memory of her helps him to conquer them; for if while wandering in the wilderness his tremulous state can finally dissolve into a vision of her form, in her white robes flitting before him smiling and beckoning, he knows the crisis is over for the time and he can return home to his duties. Thus her love does become a cure, as she maintained it would.

The remarkable thing about this story is that the sufferer, as regarded by the popular belief, is not an insane man telling his hallucinations, but an extraordinary being, a poet, a visionary, who communicates with a world of which the ordinary mortal has no conception. He has an extra window in his consciousness that opens upon other fields of life.

This belief is particularly prevalent in the more Northern part of the country where the wild magnificent sea with all its mystery and all its terror and beauty sends countless fancies into a sensitive mind. There are a hundred tales of how in the hour of one's death the sea reveals its strange wonders; how the ghost of the water—cold Death in a fisherman's garb— sails beside one in a boat which is but half; how the water chuckles and the secret depths yawn as if ready to swallow their victim. On land other strange beings exercise their power and beguile the unwary. Such mysterious stories of the influence exerted upon man by nature in her violence or her gentleness appear in the myths of every people; but such general belief in the peculiar faculty of seeing these agencies *revealed* is probably nowhere found so abundantly and so distinctly and beautifully expressed. Our folklore no less than our popular belief is rich in tales of these second-sighted men and women. Many have been introduced into literature proper through a series of volumes collected from the inexhaustible storehouse of the popular imagination.

It is a well-known fact that Christianity and its essential character, namely its spiritual teaching, did not penetrate to the innermost recesses of the Germanic mind till the time of the Reformation. The effect of its teaching before that time was mainly to create among the people in general a great deal of superstitious belief in powers hostile to Christianity rather than belief in Christianity itself. The old gods, Odin, Thor, and Tyr, with their large following, had had in the main to give way before the victorious Christ. They had quitted the scene of action, the broad daylight, and had withdrawn into the shadow. They had been banished to the caves of the earth, the deep hollows and bosom of the mountains; but they were not dead. They continued their existence in deeper mystery. They came forth when the sun had gone down, when the moon had risen and the night ruled the earth; or they appeared before certain persons who possessed the strange gift of seeing the action of invisible beings. To these they might afford great entertainment by their pranks; often they rewarded devotion by protection and assistance; but they also punished faithlessness or negligence with equal misfortune, with sickness unto death or perpetual darkening of the intellect. Prediction of the future plays a part in this strange intercourse between the fallen gods and the mortal to whom they are friendly and who still believes in their power. This prophecy is the form taken by the belief in second-sight in certain inner districts of the country where the mountains and the forests still seem to bear witness to the struggle between the Jotun and the fierce Thor, or Odin with his broadbrimmed hat.

Another kind of belief in second-sight, less related to the old paganism and more to the personal consciousness, is the seeing of the *alter ego* as a kind of pursuing evil influence. Of this, however, I know no instance in existing literature. It appears only in popular legend.

GRIEG AS A NATIONAL COMPOSER

ERTAIN criticism of the music of Grieg, while generally appreciative of his technical skill and lenient to his peculiarities, nevertheless plainly declares him to have fallen short of being a great musician—that is, one who treats themes of universal interest and whose ideas expand into the breadth of a symphony. The prevalence of the "national" element in his music is referred to as an instance of his limited lyrical and subjective temperament, which has seized upon the narrow field of folk-song and dance as a convenient and natural vehicle for personal peculiarities. Such misconception may arise from the point of view from which foreigners and theorists regard the peculiarly intimate element in Grieg's music. There is, perhaps, no great necessity for correcting it, since it must in course of time inevitably correct itself; but it is a curious sign of increasing scholasticism among critics, some of whom should know from personal experience what part the national element plays in the general development of all art, and not least in music. It may thus not be useless to attempt, for the benefit of the music-loving public, a more liberal, less dogmatic appreciation of the national element in Grieg's music, and possibly also to dispel some of the false conceptions and imperfect explanations which are so often associated with the work of a composer, and are allowed to

A Late Picture of Grieg

grow and become a tradition without question as to their genuineness or likelihood.

That Grieg should be thus criticised is nothing wonderful. No doubt, when a composer becomes popular his days are, musically speaking, numbered. And Grieg has become popular; more, however, by virtue of his idiosyncrasies, his mannerisms, than by appreciation of the intrinsic value of his music. People play his pieces and gloat over them who do not understand their chief trait. This piano-playing age seizes upon anything that sounds enticing to the ear and brings out the qualities of the instrument; but what does this signify? Not by any means that the essence of the composition is always taken into account, assimilated or rendered. The outside features, the musical tricks, the phrasing, are the things grasped. By degrees, the peculiarities at first charming and even seductive become stale, and the hapless musician is reproached for possessing what was previously accounted his virtue. So it has happened to all the individual composers from Weber to Schumann—lately to Franz and Grieg; and so it will happen to all who are still the idols of the concert-room, Tschaikowsky, Dvorák and the rest. Nor is this their fault. They have all, each in turn, expressed in their individual way the conceptions prevailing in their time, and it is the fate of all things made by mortals that time, as it constantly moves on to the morrow, forgets what was of yesterday. Nor can it be made a matter of reproach that the artist has chosen for himself some small sphere of

expression wherein he moves supreme. Not the rendering of the macrocosm, in its constantly increasing vast-
ness and manifoldness, can be the aim of his art, but
only the microcosm, the world within himself, his circle,
his nation. To be rendered at all, the universe must
still be moderate in size and limited in its comprehen-
siveness, as it was in Beethoven's days, a world full
of human force which broke itself against the bars of
destiny; or it must be the universe reduced to its meta-
physical entity, as it exists in Brahms' learned and
philosophical work.

The variety of methods of human expression in which
the microcosm can be rendered has given rise to such
rather artificial standards of judging a composition
as whether it is universal or personal, objective or
subjective, epic or lyric, or even didactic or divertive
in tone. Letting these criteria stand for what they
may, what is it that, irrespective of skill of workman-
ship, ease, or learning, makes the lasting quality of a
musical work and establishes the final judgment of its
value? Is it not the predominance in it either of
thought or of feeling—the exquisitely melodious quality, spontaneous, direct, lucid; or the weighty, discur-
sive, sometimes even argumentative, utterance which
by degrees builds up the final issue and presses the
idea home? Between these two poles—exclusiveness of
thought on the one hand and expansiveness of emotion
on the other; mountain-heights of pure vision and
sheltered glades of sweet repose; the speculative quality,
"*die verstandesthätigkeit*," and the compassion charged

[148]

with memory but remote from pain—all music of aspiration wavers; sometimes touching the one, sometimes
both, sometimes remaining between. Although some
would characterize the one as the more universal and
objective, the other as the more individual and subjective expression, is it really worth while or even possible
to say which is the best and the highest? Music, as
the fluctuating expression of man's moods, can hardly
be restricted to any formula or domain of utterance.
This would be to deprive it of its greatest virtue, that
of being responsive and sympathetic to all phases of
life, to all shades of sentiment. In the end, does not
our choice depend upon our individual disposition, and
does not all music really begin, in its expression as well
as in its appreciation, with the individual? If the artist
pictures the elusive thing we call life, with its thousand
mirages, or the majestic mountain-top, where the cool
blue visions tell of immovable heights even more sub-
lime, who shall say which is the more perfect?

It has been asserted, somewhat dogmatically, that
Grieg's music has none of the objective value of the
impersonal expression which characterizes the highest
art, and that he is singularly individual, at most only
national. But in their use of the word "national," his
critics seem too narrow. Why always look upon the
national as identical with the local? The national is
not merely an expansion of the personal, it is likewise a
step toward the universal; thus it unites both the objective and the subjective, the epic and the lyric. This
distinction, however, often indulged in, between the indi-

vidual and the universal, seems a mere play with words, sometimes only a question of change of opinion. No doubt, Mozart and Schubert, and Beethoven most of all, appeared distressingly subjective to their contemporaries; yet to us, whom by their individual rendering they have helped to reach a higher level of comprehension, they are universal. Such music as Scarlatti's and Bach's, because of its singleness of feeling, might be characterized as universal in the primitive sense of the word; and yet, although these men employed generally the same means and methods, they are not only in name but in individuality separate, in a sense that characterizes one as German, the other as Italian. All composers of note have either expressed some degree of national reaction against foreign influence, or have sought in their work to interpret some phase of the national temperament to the nation itself. Thus even Brahms, in spite of his cool heights of thought which might stamp him as universal to a peculiar degree, has found his chief glory in expressing not only national exaltation in the hour of grief and memory, but also the peculiar spiritual problems with which the superior minds of his nation wrestle today—the eternal riddle of a true and worthy life, the single-minded devotion to a noble idea, the sacrifice of success in order to tend the light of superior knowledge; problems which, as Brahms presents them, are more thoroughly German than they are or could be English, French, or American.

Whatever, then, the individual critic may consider the essential meaning of universal or national, it seems necessary to admit that the importance of a composer must, first of all, rest on the message he brings to his people. His natural relation is to them rather than to humanity at large, and his music becomes universal only through voicing their aspirations and character. His message to the world can have genuine force and vitality only as it is filtered through his message to his nation. In Europe nationality has for too long a time been a latent and potent force not to exert influence even over an art which, like music, may claim to have cosmopolitan tendencies.

It seems that critics in their estimation of Grieg's music have often allowed themselves to be unduly influenced by his personal appearance, and measuring the one by the other have found both wanting in such strength as the normally developed is presumed to possess. That psychological reasoning which bases an estimate of mental worth on physical singularities, in which the French have of late shown themselves especially proficient, is too easy and too cheap a trick to deserve much comment. To give the accidental the force of an axiom has always been looked upon as both unphilosophical and unscientific. The utter tactlessness of the remarks showered upon Grieg—that he is a dwarf, that one shoulder is higher than the other, etc., as if this had anything to do with his efficiency as a musician!—inevitably lowers the tone of the criticism containing them.

One critic, in speaking of Grieg's use of national music, calls such music a dialect rather than a language.

The remark may, indeed, apply to the original random
tunes and lays. But the artistic treatment of these
national melodies, the elaboration of primitive har-
monies and the use of them as *motifs* on which to build
a structure of learned musical composition take away
their original crudeness and abruptness without des-
troying their characteristics, and add these forgotten
and secluded tunes to the great family of melodies with
which the whole world may become familiar. Under
such treatment, their limited exclusiveness exists no
more, and a new chapter is added to the volume of
human expression. Hence if a national composer
becomes popular in a cosmopolitan sense, as Grieg has,
this is due not merely to idiosyncrasies, but also to the
good and legitimate reason that the message he brings
is understood and appreciated by nations not akin to
his.

Grieg's position toward his country is peculiar. Of
course, other composers all over the world have made
national music theirs, worked it over, drawn inspiration
from it, feasted on its freshness of feeling, and embodied it in their works. Indeed, the national element
concealed in modern music is much larger than people
would at first be inclined to believe. Nay, upon exami-
nation the national element will show itself influential
even in cases where the composer alone is credited with
the invention of his melodies. But, however successful
in their application of the national, none, from Weber
to Tschaikowsky, has been so completely in sympathy
with its nature, so obedient to its character, its form

and color, as has Grieg. Many see in this a distinct
limitation of his genius. Grieg ought to have done as
his brethren did, they think. He should have treated
the national material as a makeshift, as an interpola-
tion or ornament. But this has not been natural to
him to do, and the result seems to justify his attitude.
What the possession of a national music such as his
means to a people, the value of its stimulating and
unifying power, Americans, who do not as yet possess
any, cannot quite understand. It is the same with the
man who does not know what fatherhood is until he himself has a child. While the music which claims to be
universal expresses often the merest generalities, is
vague, indefinite and theoretical—"attenuated cos-
mopolitanism," as Carlyle puts it—national music is
strong, direct, alive in every fibre. It is of enormous
educational influence to the people, bringing the ideas
all have in common home to their mind and heart, with
the strength of what is home-grown and truly lived.

Of all the Norwegian composers of national music,
none has touched, as Grieg has, the spring of the
idiomatically national. The mountain fairy of whom
Norwegian folklore tells, the mysterious spirit of the
voices of the forest and the silence of the glens, the
golden-haired and blue-eyed maiden, Muse of the peasants and inspirer of their lays, she who appears in the
solitude and plays the "*langelek*" and "*lur*," of whom
the poets have sung eloquently but abstractly,—she
revealed herself at last in all her eerie power, when
Grieg took these "boorish" tunes and lent them a voice

that could reach farther than the faint vibration and whispering of her fantastic cithern. Thus Norwegian peasant-music has reached a development which it could not otherwise get, has become what it now is—bizarre, often morbid, sometimes boisterously gay, full of wild grace, taunting and jeering, yet plaintive and brooding; always singular, forceful and brilliant. Norwegians did not realize what possibilities were in them or their songs until Grieg put his hand to the elaboration of these tunes.

When I here apply the word "national" to the Norwegian peasant-music as it originally existed, I ought perhaps to do so with a certain reservation. It may be that there is no such thing as strictly national music; nothing in its beginning is quite home-grown, everything is somehow transmitted from elsewhere and then assimilated. In fact, several of the Norwegian folk-tunes, for instance, in their beautiful sensitiveness suggest strongly both Haydn and Bach, or even remoter sources. In the same way, the Swedish "polska" in its vivacity, mocking charm and martial clamor forcibly reminds one of Slavic folk-tunes. But whatever was the musical germ of these songs and dances, they have been so thoroughly recast according to the popular temperament that today they are Norwegian; and by Grieg's working of them into the mould of more universal tendencies, they are also in the broadest sense national.

Nor is it only the national in its ethnological meaning, but also the background of national feeling, of

[154]

patriotism, the historical past recorded in song and tale which have been voiced by Grieg as they have never been voiced before and perhaps never will be again. It is necessary only to remember Sonata, Opus 7, with the meditative, almost religious, Andante, the majestic Menuetto and the fiery Finale, which maintains its proud bearing to the end and closes with strains of highest enthusiasm and assurance. When one compares the Menuetto with compositions of romantic and patriotic tenor, such as Chopin's Polonaise No. 7, Opus 53, one meets with the same reference to a heroic past. In Chopin's Polonaise, we have history brilliant and exhilarated by blares of trumpets, by beauty and valor, by the glamor of a great gathering, by the tramp of horses and the flash of swords, until, by a subtle change of mood, it all sinks into dust and the night-wind moans gently over forgotten graves. Grieg's Menuetto suggests no sense of bereavement, but a continuous and proud presence of the fairest and noblest of the land, crowned with strength and beauty—a throng of knights and dames, lords and ladies, the throne in the background, and the standards of many battles and adventures waving in the summer-breeze, while the torches glow and the music, now majestic, urging to deed, now gentle, persuading to pleasure, puts the crowd in motion responsive to its rhythm. If to this we add Grieg's music to Björnson's poems and dramas, which are epic if anything, his compositions for choruses and orchestra in which he has lent the poetic words a wonderful, soul-speaking power, his witty rendering of portions of

Peer Gynt and his *Holberg Suite,* we find he has expressed for his nation its greatest good of all: the feeling of its historical integrity and its oneness with the land that bore it. Such beautiful patriotism, never maudlin or chauvinistic, frank, earnestly devoted with a son's devotion, will suggest that he sank his own individuality in the larger unit, rather than that he made the national subservient to himself.

It is, perhaps, not altogether wrong to say that the bane of Grieg's highest work was his settling for good in his villa by Bergen and secluding himself from the vigorous life elsewhere. Certainly, if one knows the temperamental likeness between himself and Mozart, whose ethereal and unworldly height of beauty and feeling he rendered as no one else does, and his strong musical leanings toward Schumann, it is clear that not all he had to say is embodied in the national. He wished to express other things, which with unimpaired health, a different environment, and greater means, he might perhaps triumphantly have said. Possibly, as has been declared, Grieg did not develop into the most powerful expression, into grappling with cosmic problems and solving them in symphonies. Yet the time-honored custom of considering a composer of but middling worth until he has foisted his aspiration to immortality upon the world in the shape of a symphony, is about as fallacious as the eighteenth-century theory that whoever had not written an opera was really no musician of note. It reminds one of the English literary notion that a poet who has not written a drama, however lame dramatically, is no great poet. Grieg struck the pole of feeling rather than the pole of thought. And within the sphere of national feeling, at least, he surely combined the opposite elements, voicing the epic and objective as well as the lyric and subjective. In fact, the two are in him so curiously blended that, contrary to current opinion, it is the nation which speaks its innermost thoughts through Grieg's music as much as Grieg himself. We agree that he was more of an artist in his production than a philosopher. Hence, according to the demands of some æsthetic rigorists, he failed to reach the very highest rank. But a composer is not made up according to a pattern, a universal pattern; he is made according to something which it is in his nature to become. Grieg with his opportunities and endowment appears to have made the most of both, to have expressed what he found most worth expressing with such surpassing beauty and oneness of feeling that the nation for which he did this owes his work an infinite debt of affection and esteem.

PERSONAL RECOLLECTIONS OF GRIEG

September 5, 1907

GAIN Norway has lost one from among her circle of great sons and daughters. Edward Grieg is dead. The circle is growing smaller as the names that have been intimately associated with her rise from an unknown country to a leading position in the world of literature and art disappear from the list of the living. Grieg (born in 1843) lived to be over sixty years old, the greater part of his manhood being spent on his property near Bergen, where he composed a large portion of his piano pieces. It is said that his health was not of the best, but his joy in his work was not therefore any less. Up to his very last years he issued songs and piano compositions, besides giving concerts both at home and abroad and contributing with his pen to the musical and biographical literature of our day.

Grieg has somewhere told the story of his early youth and his studies. He came of a musical family, his mother being especially gifted, and from her he received his first instruction. He soon began to compose and dreamed of going to study in Germany. But it was considered a great risk to send so young a boy away from home alone, and Ole Bull was the one who persuaded the anxious parents that the son was really deserving of so great a sacrifice. In Leipsic he was

Grieg in 1879

brought up in the traditions of Schumann, Mendelssohn, and Chopin; and like Kjerulf he might never have found the true medium for his musical gifts if—by an accident—the treasure hidden in the old Norwegian folksongs had not been revealed to him. Through these he saw the path for him to follow. He adopted their form, but the speech was after all his own. Even the form, under his dexterous sensitive handling, assumed undreamed of musical possibilities. For Grieg was a great artificer, a master of harmony, a thorough judge of musical means, a painter who wielded a very suggestive brush. On the Continent he was for a long time known as the Chopin of the North. But his world was one of more freedom, of less retrospection, than was that of the great Pole. He was more imbued with the spirit of adventure and conquest and exultation in the promised land within his sight, than could ever have been the wonderful Polish romanticist, whose soul brooded over splendors and powers that were lost and vanquished.

Few nations have greeted a composer with more instantaneous appreciation than the Norse people gave to Grieg's early works. We felt with one accord that in his pieces was voiced a spirit at once national, historic, yet thoroughly modern; and we were proud to call it our own. Grieg has remained our interpreter until this day. His compositions gave us a hearing and allowed our most seductive melodies to win friends for us all over the world. Where Grieg is, there is

Norway; and sad will be the regret with which the news of his death will everywhere be received.

The first time I met Grieg was on one autumn day in 1879. He had come to Christiania in the spring of that year and his fame as conductor and teacher had already made him an instructor much sought. I have always remembered his courteous greeting and smile of welcome. He was a very small man, delicately built, slender as a boy, but with a rather large head surmounted by a crown of glorious blond hair. His hands, too, were very large, as a pianist's should be, strong and yet shapely. As was proper, I had to sit down and play for him— one of his own compositions. He said I did pretty well but not so well as the composition deserved. My method was at fault. To eradicate the failings would be an endless task, hence I had better begin from the very beginning. And I began that day with five-finger exercises, for Grieg meant what he said. The next time I went he gave me one of Mozart's sonatas, and it was then that he played for me for the first time. I have never heard any one play in a manner so instinct with the very soul of music (that most heavenly and illusive of all arts) as did Grieg. His eyes, which were generally of an almost colorless blue, underwent a change when he played; a fire sprang up in them, they became suffused with a light such as is born only in those who see the heavens open before their rapt gaze. His face and whole being radiated inspiration and response of soul and body to the voices that arose under his fingers. I have never heard and shall never again hear any one play Mozart—that divine master now so little appreciated—as Grieg did; with phrasing so exquisite and such complete command of the beauties of melody. At such moments genius undoubtedly spoke to genius, and I was many times privileged to be near and hear.

Grieg was most ardently beloved by his pupils. When he gave concerts they flocked to hear and applaud him. Wherever he went a train of devoted disciples escorted him to and from the railroad station, gave him three times three cheers, flowers, smiles, and adoring glances. And Grieg enjoyed it. Even when most tired, he brightened at once into radiant sunshine and no smile could be more responsive, warmer, or more enthusiastic than his. Yet he was not a teacher to be trifled with. The tallest and sturdiest stood in awe of him when he conducted an orchestra or sat down at the piano. He soon did away with mannerisms such as the tyro is inclined to adopt for the sake of effect. A reproof from his lips when some awkward passage irritated him was something everyone dreaded and recoiled from. There was much grief in Christiania when after a stay of a year and a half he decided to return to his birthplace, Bergen. That was the last I saw of him, but the memory of him as a musician and an interpreter is forever with me, as with all his pupils.

THE CATHEDRAL AT TRONDHJEM*

and A VISION OF THE PAST, *(1885)*

LYING near the southeast corner of Trondhjem* is the famous cathedral, the old Christ Church—gray with age, a world by itself, whence a breath from the thoughts and struggles of the past comes with impressive greeting. Though weatherbeaten and broken, the church is unique in our land both for its architectural beauty and for its suggestion of history and legend. If we stand on the high fortification of the town in a late autumn afternoon, the evening star already visible, and gaze down at the old city lying between the pale blue sea and the mountains, the sight of the great old church centered among numberless little dark-colored houses carries us far back to the middle ages. Two amiable figures from the hoary past—Saga and Myth—seem to sit within its leaning walls and whisper tales of the glories of its palmy days. The dark masses of its spires and towers point up admonishingly, and the gathering fog, moving in drifts here and there, seems like ghostly armies of forefathers brooding still over their old abiding place, wandering through its time-worn streets, and hovering over the crosses in the churchyard as if to rebuke them for being half buried in sleep and weary of telling the living

*Pronounced Trŏnyĕm. The restoration of the cathedral has continued since 1885 and is now almost complete.—ED.

Trondhjem Cathedral, Restored

Trondhjem Cathedral, Before Restoration

where the dead lie. Even the fortification, with its grass-covered ramparts and grim arsenal watched by one lone sentinel, seems only like a Shade of the past.

With the recognition after his death of Olav Haraldsson as the patron saint of Norway, Olav's shrine became a national treasure to be preserved, and the little Christ Church then standing over St. Olav's grave became the treasure house. It was the small beginning of the present cathedral. Slowly it added to its dignities and increased its dimensions, showing many variations of style in its different periods of growth, till finally it stood as near completion as it ever was, the largest and most richly embellished cathedral of the North, with St. Olav's shrine of weighty silver placed on the high altar as "the crown and pride of the land."

Then came losses. Early in the fourteenth century it was almost demolished by fire. Other fires at intervals, tempests, war, the Black Death, wasted the church and the land;—the ravages of the church seeming but an outer sign of that inner impotence which depleted the life of Norway itself. At the coming of the Reformation the last archbishop fled and took with him the chief treasure, St. Olav's shrine, thus violating the sanctity of the church. The innermost casket of heavy silver, set with jewels and containing the bones of the saint, was snatched away and carried to Copenhagen where it was made into bullion. Other possessions were stolen and the revenues of the church stopped. When the Swedish Protestant military invaded the city they used the ruinous but yet stately old building as a stable.

They ran off with the body of St. Olav as a special trophy and buried it near the Swedish border.

In the following centuries little by little restorations were made, temporary and tasteless efforts, showing sad poverty both of money and of love. Finally in 1869 a complete and efficient restoration was begun and is being continued at the present day. Whether near or distant, the church is of mighty proportions and imposing. It lies like an elongated cross stretching from West to East, with short broad wings. The West nave is in ruins, the East now restored.

Of all the work of restoration so far done, the chancel has been the most difficult and is the most beautiful. Like a precious stone lying in its perfection amid a quantity of sand and loose earth, the chancel and its adjacent finished portions are at present found quiet and intact, though close neighbor to a mass of debris and a noisy confusion of workmen and machinery. It is separated from the nave by a special entrance and steps and has its own particular groined ceiling. Over the portal is a beautiful marble figure of Christ. All the art of the style, in this as in many other cathedrals, is concentrated in the chancel; the beauty of pillars and vaults and the striving upward of the long pointed arches give it distinction and set it apart as a sacred place dedicated to the high altar and to services held on the most solemn occasions. The shrine of St. Olav was and is here in the chancel directly opposite the spot where the saint was buried. Near it is St. Olav's Well, also an important relic; while the adjoining

The Nave and Chancel

chapels and chapter houses form a chain of important buildings in the closest connection with the chancel, the holy of holies. Just as the chancels of many foreign cathedrals possess superb dimension and architectural grandeur beyond the rest of the building, so this chancel possesses an unsurpassed wealth and delicacy of detail The whole is a great piece of lacework, embroidery in stone. Besides, the airy lightness characteristic of Gothic architecture is here and elsewhere in this church emphasized by the slender white marble pillars that mark the corners and run upward to the arches of the clerestory and the rich masses of the triforium. Everywhere in the building they appear and create a cheerful brightness, glittering like new-fallen snow from their background of soft gray soapstone. Seen against the massive pillars, they recall the white trunks of birch trees amid a forest of dark pine. The likeness of the chancel to a forest glade is strengthened too, by a wealth of plant forms, leaf ornaments, garlands, wreathed and branched arches.

The beauty of these finished portions makes a visitor all the more eager to see the great West nave with its historic King's Entrance restored to its splendor. Even now, despite all its confusion as a workshop, no portion of the church expresses such power and purity of style. The clearness and restfulness of line triumph over all the injury and awaken that delight which is ever the reward of the truest art.

At present the mingling of old and new in the church diminishes the pleasure of observing it. One's happiest impression is gained by lamplight, when a reconciling veil is thrown over what is unfinished and crude and when the warm gray in the color of the walls, which makes them look extraordinarily venerable in daytime, brightens under the light of sconces and chandeliers into a transparent clearness. A glad festive air then fills the place. The Christ figure shines out white against the illumined background, the red velvet on the altar cloth and communion rail catches the light, and forth from the dimness of the corners the apostles seem to step with their emblems—St. John and St. Peter stand near the altar, St. Paul leans on his sword, while St. Bartholomew raises his hand to proclaim the gospel.

A Vision of the Past

One evening as I sat quite alone absorbed in the beauty just described of this strangely spirited scene, the great building underwent before my eyes a marvelous transformation. Every suggestion of ruin and repair was gone, and with it all the bareness characteristic of a Protestant church. It stood complete and perfect, decorated and beautiful, rich and homelike, as in the days when it was the one centre of the community life. Its recesses were filled with altars and draperies, its niches with statues; paintings and tapestries occupied its wall spaces, while in the windows were images which I knew shed glowing color upon the blackness outside. Transfixed with wonder, I started violently when trudging steps as of sandalled

The King's Entrance

feet and a bent figure wrapt in a long black robe approached the chancel. A horn lantern was placed on the steps, the portal unlocked, and as the figure moved in I saw the light fall on his gray bald head. After a moment he came out again carrying a missal. His look passed over me unseeing, but fear drove me back into the shadow. Then he knelt, as he had forgotten to do before entering, and knelt again, laboriously, with creaking joints and guarding himself from dropping the book, made the double cross, again passed me unseeing, and slowly shambled off.

I had risen to my feet strangely shaken. But now the deep sound of bells filled the room, wonderfully solemn, the bells of vesper service. Music began from the organ, and a procession of white-clad figures small and large approached, their censers swaying like red dots. Before entering the chancel all knelt. At the altar the bishop knelt again, then turned and showed his monstrance. A small bell tinkled. Beneath the altar-vaulting, shaped like a great ciborium, glittered St. Olav's silver shrine. Then from the throng of worshippers who had silently gathered in the stretches of the church came low reverberations:

Ave Maria, mater Dei, ora pro nobis,
Sancte Olave, qui es in coelis . . .

Faces and forms in quick succession pressed forward to reach the sanctuary and receive the sacrament from the hands of the bishop.

Presently the multitude swayed and parted. Through it was carried a sick pilgrim who sought penance and healing on this festival day from St. Olav. On the floor he lay, his dying glance fixed on the altar shrine. The bishop knelt beside him, made the sign of the cross over him, sprinkled him with holy water from St. Olav's Well, breathed upon him, took both his hands in his, and finally spread over him a cloth which had covered the body of the saint and thus acquired miraculous power. He then returned to the altar and prayed in silence.

All eyes were on the sick man. Presently he began to move, cast the cover aside and strove to sit up. The bystanders seemed unable to come to his help. They were too astonished to believe that their eyes were witnessing a miracle. But the bishop cried out, "Help him, you who are hale and hearty, wonderful powers have descended upon him!" Then there was great agitation. They cried aloud, they wept, they fell on their knees and praised God. All gathered around to get a raveling of the miraculous cloth or even to touch it; and many arms lent their strength to lead the sick one across the floor to the bishop, who laid hands upon them. With the healed one all knelt, called upon the saints for their special needs, and made their vows. In the midst was the half sinking healed one, almost beside himself, happy and tired. The bishop read the confession of faith for the whole congregation, read the blessing, took the cup, and followed by tapers, crosses, and incense, proceeded from the church. The healed one was lifted up and carried out, a faint glow of convalescence on his cheeks.

* * * * * *

With the procession, departed all light and life. I
scarcely knew where I was.

A chilly gust passed through the dark church, and
the silence was oppressive. Slowly the place was illumined by a faint ominous light. It was still the gor-
geous church, but it was so empty, so black, so full of
fears. A dull mumbling was heard, and up in the place
for proclaiming the banns appeared Master Erik, the
Blind, the Fearful. He had his archbishop's mitre on
his head and carried his curved staff. About him stood
twelve priests with burning tapers. All intoned hymns
of lamentation. The archbishop lifted his staff high in
the air and cried out into the church:

"Anathema!

In the name of the Father, the Son, and the Holy
Ghost, as well as in the name of the mild unblemished
Virgin Mary and all the holy saints,

We excommunicate,

Not alone by the right which our seat grants us but
also supported by God's own word and Peter's power
to bind and release in heaven and on earth,

Thee, King of Norway, Sverre Sigurdsson,

A tool of the devil, a traitor to bishop, priests, and
the whole people of Norway.

And with thee all those who have followed thee, supported thee, recognized thee as king and thy actions
as just.

Be they all cast out of the lap of the church and
condemned to eternal punishment."

A prolonged sigh of anguish went through the
church; and again the heart-rending hymns of lamenta-

tion. The bishop once more lifted his staff and pronounced the banns over the congregation, yea, over all the inhabitants of the land.

"Cursed be thy activity in the state,
Cursed be thou in the fields,
Cursed be thy savings,
Cursed be thy descendants,
Cursed be thy lifework,
Cursed be thy coming in and thy going out,

Upon thee come all the curses that Moses enumerates and upon thee be the righteous Anathema Maranatha, which is: that ye be made to naught by the second visitation of our Lord.

No one will say to thee 'God's Peace'; no priest read the mass or administer the Lord's Sacrament.

As cattle shall ye be buried and your bodies shall crumble upon the earth.

And as the torches in our hands are now extinguished, so shall your lights be extinguished, as surely as ye do not render to God's Church full penance and compensation.

Anathema!"

The torches were reversed and put out. "Anathema" was whispered round about, "Amen" was responded, "Be done as is said." . . .

Sweat stood upon my brow. I seemed to be at the bottom of a grave. My God! Was there no one any more, were they all slain by the curse? Did the church lie full of corpses?. . . Ghostly voices seemed to call around me: "Cry out, if there be any one to hear thee. To whom of the holy saints will ye turn?" . .

"No, no hope, only horror, O horror! For the cursed no place is sanctified, no happiness, no peace, no consolation." . . .

"Do penance! Offer all that you have! Nothing is so great that peace of mind is not far greater." . .

. . .

Darkness enveloped me.

* * * * * *

Then suddenly there was a loud knock at the church portal. Again a knock. "Open the church portal," some one shouted. "The right authority, the Lord's own anointed, King Sverre Sigurdsson, stands without! He does not bear the sword in vain!"

The tumult soon put life into the dead bones. From the arches to the nave, lights burst forth. Steps resounded loudly from all directions. More lights flared up. There was a jingling of keys and clash of weapons. The King was in the church! I heard his voice.—"The monarchy is ordained according to the command of God, not according to the device of man. No one receives the kingdom but by dispensation of divine Providence—"

A host of clergy came with the crucifix and placed themselves at each side of the entrance to the chancel. But the King continued: "Does a clergy, priest or archbishop, cardinal or pope, dare to declare God's own chosen excommunicated, and to condemn them who

[171]

follow him, when he served God in his kingdom, not himself?"

At this voices filled the room with loud singing. Lights were everywhere.

"God alone sees the heart!" shouted the King. "His judgment is righteous. Therefore it happens that one bound by the Church can stand free before God!"

A glory as of the midday sun filled the church, while the singing grew louder and higher, like a devout invocation and exultant thanksgiving.

* * * * * *

Then King Sverre was no longer present. His grandson, King Haakon, entered with his bodyguard and highborn men. Before him strode Archbishop Sigurd with his pallium, the priests of the chapter following and carrying crucifixes and banners. Now the lights of the high altar were also burning. I saw the antependium wrought in gold, the vast treasure of golden vessels and relics, and upon the altar cloth the costly shrine, glittering with many precious stones. On the steps knelt my hero of the sagas, Haakon, the greatest and most fortunate of Norway's kings, invoking the aid of St. Olav. The archbishop himself was praying before the altar.

* * * * * *

But as he communed there, lifting his eyes towards the crucifix, it was no longer Sigurd, but Archbishop Jon, praying alone, thirty-two years later, and bidding farewell to his seat and his dreams. . . All

The Cathedral in Winter

the glory had vanished. . . The galleries lay in
darkness. . . Not a sound was heard. . . The
lights were out. Only before St. Olav's shrine burned
two torches, and out in the nave glimmered like a distant spark a single light here and there before the image
of a saint. And the Archbishop still knelt in the silent
church, praying low.

* * * * * *

Then suddenly there was a frightened shout:—
"Christ Church is burning!" Heavy smoke filled the
nave. Flames issued here and there. Doors were
thrown open and a multitude of people rushed in.
Through the corridors and naves they ran back and
forth and up and down the stairways. The archbishop
tried to direct them. The priests did what they could.
Pails of water were carried to the upper galleries and
dashed upon the flames. Ladders were hoisted to the
fiercest fire. Below in the church relics and vessels
were seized for safety, tapestries were torn from the
walls, and images of saints were carried away or by
accident dashed to pieces. In the midst of the anxiety,
water, smoke, noise, and despair, a little flock of
believers knelt at the entrance to the chancel and prayed
for the preservation of the church. But it continued
to burn. At last St. Olav's shrine was lifted from the
altar to be carried out. Just then the first stones from
the vaulting fell. Terrible confusion followed. The
ladders were torn down. Shrieks and moans from those
in the galleries sounded throughout the church. All
rushed toward the doors. St. Olav's shrine could

[173]

scarcely be taken out through the crowd. A hollow thud was heard, followed by thundering. The roof was falling in.

* * * * * *

I started to escape with the rest. But a skeleton rose before me and cried: "Now is the Day of Judgment!"

Unable to evade it, I slipped and lay headlong among the smoldering smoking ruins.

* * * * * *

Agnes Mathilde Wergeland
1913

foreign language or of appealing to a people rapidly
changing and from whom many continuous years of
residence abroad almost completely severed her. Yet
she never lost the longing for expression of the deep
inner self that sought an æsthetic form. She herself
said that when she had given up hope of attainment in
music, in color and line, she turned to words and to the
words of her mother tongue as a precious medium still
left her. But poverty, foreign living, and the need
of following an arduous profession to supply the daily
requirements—such conditions may easily be too heavy
to allow the maturing, in art-forms, of even the greatest talents.

Besides, Dr. Wergeland was a scholar and a teacher;
and it may be that the eminence she gained in these,
possibly more prosaic fields, was itself a reason for the
incomplete growth in the purely artistic. At any rate,
it would be injudicious to say that the world lost by
the fact that more than song, poem, or landscape, she
produced authoritative investigations in history and
led many young men and women to perceive new values
in study and new beauties and dignities in life. Her
work after all was the same, though through different
means, as the work of her famous relatives. It was the
uplifting, light-bearing, man-loving task of the pioneer-
poet and the pioneer-novelist. If she reached less fame,
that is partly because the world sets an excessively high
value on the moulding of ideas as seen in sentences,
colors, and clays, and an excessively low value on the

BIOGRAPHICAL NOTE

HE writer of the foregoing essays, Agnes Mathilde Wergeland, possessed no small measure of the talents belonging to her family. Full of poetical feeling and delicate intuitional judgment, sensitive to all beauty in nature and in art, with tastes highly trained, she seemed to those who knew and loved her best always on the verge of doing, in some art-form, greater things than she had yet done She herself felt that her art impulses had even from childhood been hindered and checked; and this was no doubt true. What she might have done in music could she have continued to study under such instruction as Grieg's, whose high praise she won, can only be conjectured. Her passion for music, her love for her piano, and the fire of inspiration that often flashed up in her when she played it, were something to witness. Her attempts in painting and drawing showed great natural ability—left untaught. Perhaps her ability was unduly sacrificed to the gift of her brother, who became a noted painter,* and for whose education she and her mother stinted themselves in the years of her girlhood. Even recently she wrote of her desire: "I long to bring forth the intimate tender picture hid away in my soul unlimned."

Her wish to write poetry was cramped by two insuperable obstacles—the necessity either of using a

*See Frontispiece. This picture is so popular that it was used as a stamp during the Centenary Celebration of 1914.—Ed.

[175]

As a Girl of Seventeen

moulding of ideas as seen in the routine teaching of human intellects and lives.

Strong as her art impulses were, it may be questioned whether she would have been satisfied with gratifying them alone. Perhaps her instinct for thought was even stronger—curiosity about the past, philosophical questioning about man, his relations, conditions, and future possibility. This led her to extensive study in the broader fields of history, civilization, economics, and culture. History of art, history of literature, were indeed vital to her and she made them truly vital to others; but she saw them in their proper perspective as only partial manifestations of the general development of the race. These truly philosophical conceptions became in time her most characteristic ideas, and they shaped and ordered the facts of every subject she studied or taught.

Even in her early girlhood she showed a strong desire for a fuller education than the ordinary by walking several miles in all weather in order to attend an academy in Christiania, and afterwards to continue her reading at the University library. As she progressed, her interests ran into unusual lines. So much so that later she chose as a thesis for her doctorate an investigation of the old Norse laws concerning legitimate birth. Some years afterwards, about 1900, she produced a study called *Slavery in Germanic Society in the Middle Ages*. This work was so excellent that she was at once recognized as the chief authority on that subject in the United States.

As is evidenced by these topics, mediæval history was the field in which she took most delight and had the greatest mastery. Her familiarity with this period is further proved by a Syllabus of Mediæval Architecture which she felt the need of and proceeded to write while she was teaching history of art at Bryn Mawr College. This work still holds a worthy place. Besides these more extensive productions, she wrote dozens of articles and book reviews for various learned journals and contributed not infrequently to Scandinavian papers, both here and in Norway.

Dr. Wergeland spent the last twenty-four years of her life in the United States. She came soon after having distinguished herself by being the first of her countrywomen to forge ahead and attain the degree of doctor of philosophy. It was granted by the University of Zürich, the only institution in Europe at that time offering the degree to women. She used a graduate fellowship in history that she won at Bryn Mawr College as a wedge to enter the scholastic world in America. She said of herself in explaining her coming that Lona Hessel in Ibsen's *Pillars of Society* had for years been to her a kind of model and inspiration, and in a way was the cause of her plan to make a place for herself in this country. She may have found double inspiration in the fact that she knew Lona Hessel to be chiefly the creation of her great kinswoman, Camilla Collett. Lona's business in the play is to "let in the light"; and though Dr. Wergeland found darkness and much difficulty when she came to America, she also found and brought much light.

She became warmly attached to the land of her adoption. With far too keen insight and too much historical sense not to detect the errors in the operation of our governmental machinery, she yet had abundant faith in the United States, and felt the tremendous breadth of its power and future activity. But the homeland was even more dear. Exiled from it in a way as she felt herself to be, she still watched it from a distance, loved it, communed with it, and at times rebuked it. How eagerly she awaited events when the separation from Sweden took place, and how proud and thankful she was that war was then averted and that after centuries of tutelage the spirited little country was at last setting forth in its rightful career of complete self-government and national independence. But she feared for it, too, in its young independence. In an article printed in a Norse paper she expressed some of this fear and uttered a warning. Incidentally she showed the prophetic power given by her study of history when in 1911 she declared imminent almost the precise diplomatic relations and political conditions now existing in the great European war of 1914-16. How such a war would affect Norway was the point of her anxiety. On all such matters her thought was wide-reaching, penetrating, and accurate.

Dr. Wergeland was for a time connected with both Bryn Mawr College and the University of Chicago; at which institutions the present writer had the benefit of a close friendship with her. For years she remained a nonresident Extension lecturer for the University of Chicago. But the largest field for activity was opened to her in the University of Wyoming. Perhaps the self-complacent East too lightly let slip away from it what she had to give. At any rate, to the young open-minded West, where possibly the need was greater, she took the wealth of her culture and there made practical for hundreds of students a large measure of the riches of her experience and her unusual intellectual equipment.

She found in Wyoming a mental atmosphere that suited her. Always a pioneer and a radical in thought (however gentle in manner), always a keen observer of the progress of women in recent history, it was not for nothing that she taught in a university maintained by the first state in the union to grant women suffrage; not for nothing that she met and made friendships there with women who were lawyers, reformers, members of state committees, and voters on all public questions.

She became known as a speaker, too, and a public lecturer—she, the shy one, who when she first came to the country possessed little conversational English and complained of feeling like a dumb animal, "ein stummes Thier." The students were never so well pleased as when she gave them a talk in chapel or an address on some memorial day. Women's clubs throughout and beyond the state asked for her services. And when on any of these occasions she responded, the rich vein of humor and keen wit lying among her weightier quali-

Six Years Old

ties sparkled forth for the enjoyment of her listeners; and the purity and beauty of her English speech with its slightest trace of accent was always wonderingly remarked. At the time when Ibsen's fame was freshest and greatest in this country, she gave a course of Extension lectures on modern drama that attracted wide attention. All this she did, with weakening health and in the brief intervals of heavy teaching, winter and summer.

It is pleasant to think of these last years when she had won universal respect and the loving admiration of numberless students; when the weight of melancholy which darkened her youth and was indeed a family inheritance, was lightened more than it had ever been; and when she had gained and continued to gain such success as she should have had long before. Especially pleasant is it to think of the close sustaining friendship she had with one in particular of her colleagues, Grace Raymond Hebard, herself a writer on history and government, a large contributor to the intellectual life of the state, and in every way a notable woman. In this friend she found complete sympathy and a spontaneous never failing affection. To her she once wrote in English this tribute:

A Song of Thy Hand

May I sing thee, dear, a song of thy hand?
No lovelier sight shall heaven e'er send.
I see thee now as I saw thee then,
All rapt in attention forward bend

While the music rattled and muttered in storm.
But my heart sang a song of a different form.
My eye swept thee up in a motion most fleet
And kissed thy sweet self from head to feet.
Ah, never was love more tenderly near
To whisper its secret to soul and ear.
But thou spoke too, and the speaker so meek
Was the gentle hand against thy cheek;
The supple, the endlessly active hand,
Ever patient to answer each eager demand.
It has done so much and loved so much,
Has lifted great loads, smoothed paths with a touch.
As a blossom it lay against thy hair,
A white dove's wing, most peaceful and fair.
Though radiant with life, with thought and firm will,
It slept on thy cheek then, dreambound and still.
Of velvet it seemed, yet it is as of steel,
Yea! gifted with power to guide the state's weal.
'Twas an emblem of life, of life's far-reaching aim,
Life's pulsebeat of love, life's force above name.
If weary and laborworn, telling of care,
Yet 'tis great beyond words. Oh, my heart! Rest it
　　　　　　　　　there!

The two friends gradually acquired a home together,
dear to both of them, but to Dr. Wergeland, after many
years of stormtossed homelessness, some of them almost
unbelievably hard, that home was precious beyond
expression. In a Norse poem called *My Home* she
describes it, with such gladness and such unconscious
self-revelation that some of her lines are embodied

here—not indeed like the original in verse, but at least in rhythm.

My Home

Farewell, oh world! Now I place my key in the lock,
When I shut my door I shut you outside.
Here I withdraw when my day's work ends
And my mind is free for the life in myself,
For the depths within, for the quiet hour
And the silent voice that gives answer to questions.

How the teakettle sings! Its aroma how fresh,
Its social warmth giving comfort and peace
To the wornout limbs and the labored breath.

Nor am I alone in my well-loved home.
When I enter the door one greets me glad.
Long as we live, we shall not forget
Life's hills are high and better than one pull two.

Many things here I love, my watch
With its heartening tick, its admonition to work;
A zither I play, so difficult, delicate;
My pictures too, my choice of things seen and loved.
Besides, I dream of what I would do,
Had my hope come true, had I not been retarded. —
—— Out here the lines are fine, the colors are golden,
And I long to bring forth the intimate tender picture
Hid away in my soul unlimned.

And yet I am happy, how happy! within these four
walls
That are mine, my own.

When distant, always before me lived books,
And chair, and the warm red glow of the lamp.
Out on the ocean, in London, in Norway—wherever—
I longed with a heartsick wish for the little red lamp,
    For it was peace.

  And now when I sit here and read
From the writings of those I most love,
The old Greeks, and Vigny, and Shelley,
My beloved American singers,
My home is a meeting-place for countless great
    thoughts,
Happy and tender and sad, pictures of dreams,
Dwelling here in wonderful spirit and strength.
And they hearten me too—strengthen to venture more
    struggles
    Out there in the world.

With this home and this companion and the friendliest regard of the whole community, her last years had more sunshine and happiness than she had ever known. That she responded to it as a bird to the warmth of spring, is proved by the Norse poems that she wrote in these years; a few filled with sadness, but most of them outbursts of the happy singing heart within pouring forth its love for trees and flowers, the sunshine, the mountains, and above all for her beloved Norway.

But she grew physically weaker and mortally weary. She had always worked tremendously, and now for years she had greatly exceeded her strength; finding, too, the extremes of the climate and the altitude very taxing to her weakened heart. At last in the winter of 1914 an unexpected illness overtook her and carried her to the bed from which she never rose.

Afterward, beneath her pillow, was found in Norse a fantastic grim vision of what she was experiencing. The old mood of melancholy possessed her in that midnight, calling up strange dark images, and enticed her perforce to travel with it through the Shadowy Vale. But we in reading it should be unjust if we failed to remember that she was expressing—quite for herself—a mood, not a dominant sentiment, still less a rooted conviction.

CHARON FORGETFUL?

This is the time when Charon comes,
after midnight, when night is at its deepest.
My nurse sleeps calmly . . . . . .
Let her sleep. She will not hear me
when I step from my bed
and climb up into the window.
Outside the wind sighs . . . . . .
As I put one foot out, an arm seems to take me
and place me carefully down
on the bank of a great black stream.
For the whole street is become a slow-running river.
On the shore are benches where people sit to wait—
in the dark—for a boat that is to come.
There are not so few on my bench.
All of them are fully dressed.
One man carries a walking stick.

[185]

A woman is wearing a curly ostrich feather.   .   .   .
I alone have nothing but a thin night slip.
  They sit erect and stiff. I cannot see their faces—
perhaps despair is written there, or indifference,
or something that leads them to ask for death.
It may be they are dead already. .   .   .   .
  I am the only one who sits there
crouched together, with the damps of night
like a cold shroud lying on me.

  And the water yonder moves slowly. .   .   .   .   .

  This is the seventh or eighth time
I have sat out here and Charon does not come.
  What do I ask of him? Rest! Rest!
    I am so tired. .   .   .   .   .   .

  When the others get into the boat
I will try to slip in with them and go down the Styx,
and then hurry away to the land of endless sleep.
There I will roll myself together
like a poor outworn cat
in some hole or crevice where no one comes,
and at last, at last, find peace
from this throbbing, shaking heart,
this weariness, always driving, never ending.

  But   .   .   .   .   .   .   the copper! the little coin
I always lack when I need it.
Whether it falls out from between my teeth or my
      hands,

or whether my nightdress is not wet enough
to hold it fast, I do not know . . . . . .

    . . . . . And Charon is an old man.
Him we cannot deceive.
He is a man of the world too.
Every time he takes the shadows,
he sees that all happens as is fitting.
He is also an exacting man.
Nothing for nothing . . . . even in the land of
  shadows.
Alas, alas! money never clung to me.

 What do people live for?
Gold . . fame . . power . . none of these
  became mine.
Toil was for me, as for many others.
I was a common soldier.
I stood in the trenches and ranks
like my brothers and sisters.
The commandant received words of praise
and fine ribbons and medals;
but we . . . received the usual nothing . . .
 To me at bottom it matters not.

 But now I wish to sleep in peace,
not be urged and driven out again
when my limbs tremble and I cannot stand up
even to see if the little boat is finally coming. . . .

 . . . . . Is it a tiny star that glows over there,
or is it a lantern? . . . .

Ah no! it is the light of dawn! The hour
is past. The rigid shadows have vanished.
I am alone. The stream too has shrunk away.
Charon has forgotten me this night.
    My wet dress has grown dry.
I seem to feel the warmth of life's fingers upon my heart.
Out in the street I can do nothing. . . . . .
The same arm that lifted me out
again lifts me in.
    Now I am in bed, on the same pillow,
with the same covering over me,
exactly as before. . . . . . .

February twentieth.

And yet, it may happen
that I shall sail away from them
some other night, when the stream lures,
and Charon really comes alongside the shore.

March fourth.

[DISCESSIT—*March sixth.*]

APPENDIX I

COLLETT ON IBSEN'S *GHOSTS*

. . . Ibsen's drama is itself a ghost, not one of those well-known ghosts which appear in our ghost stories and about which my old father used to say, "If these spirits were only not so spiritless, so tiresome!" For Ibsen's ghost we find a parallel perhaps best in Shakespeare's repertoire of spirits, those apparitions of terror which appear as retribution, as fate, and especially in his *Hamlet*, in the King apparition which seeks a soul strong enough to bear its terrible secret. It has hitherto sought in vain. All stare at it, make the sign of the cross, and let it pass silently by. The multitude who hear of it say it is nonsense, pure imagination. But Hamlet comes, Hamlet, the doubter, the inquirer—in a word, the spirit of the age. He wishes to hear. He listens while his heart chills in his bosom, and the more he listens the more does fear give place to other feelings. He not only wishes to know the secret confided to him but he will divulge it; and he not only will divulge it but he will avenge it.

Our poet, like Hamlet, the accuser, the avenger, strikes a direct blow at hypocrisy and veneer, and tears away that worm-eaten garment of apathy and habit with which society has so long covered itself. He is the first one who has had the courage to cry out to this society "There! look at what you have chosen and crowned and daily bent your knee to—of all your old tolerant, disregarded, secreted, patronized, sinful addictions the very worst—see now how beautiful it is!"—And the hypocrisy of society shouts against the disturber and throws its stones.

(Translated from *Against The Tide.)*

Björnson

NOTE ON BJÖRNSON

Translated and Arranged

About 1857 two new tendencies began to appear in Norse literature and developed into the dominant movements of the succeeding years. The influence of folklore, which had been most active during the preceding decade, now yielded to the influence of the old saga literature and to the beginnings of a realistic development. Ibsen wrote his historical dramas based on the old sagas, Björnson appeared with his peasant stories and his historical dramas simultaneously. Both men's works were written in the modernized saga style. There has been much speculation as to who really introduced this saga style. But it may be confidently asserted that Björnson was the first to introduce it in his stories and novels *(Synnöve Solbakken)*, and Ibsen in *The Warriors* established it on the stage.

The drift toward realism, toward a study of the problems of life, appeared in Ibsen's dramatic works, in Björnson's participation in political life, and in Camilla Collett's plea for the cause of woman. Björnson threw himself with all his energy into the political turmoil; he fought for his ideas not only as a poet but as a journalist and a patriot. Camilla Collett sacrificed her purely literary career and devoted all her efforts to advocating her social ideas through treatises and newspaper articles. Ibsen alone stayed away from journalism and political agitation, but he did not turn away from his contemporaries; on the contrary, he studied conditions with zeal and energy and finally began to picture them.

Björnson is said to be the most vigorous and the most admired poetical genius of the later nineteenth century. He was the youngest of the group of writers and the most irresistible. Wherever he went, there was life, light and bustle. All gathered around him, he was born to be a centre and he immediately became so. He did not need to fight his way to his leadership; he assumed it at once, as if it were so ordained. Previous writers had described nature and had presented the folklore. To picture individuals who belonged to the people and lived in the mountain regions—that was the task Björnson undertook. His predecessors had led their readers into woods and fields and had given them some glimpses of the life of the people. But this poet opened the door to the peasant's hut, and even more to his heart. Though in other kinds of literature Björnson created original and remarkable works, his most characteristic productions are his peasant novels. *Synnöve Solbakken* was followed in time by *Arne, A Happy Boy, The Fisher Maiden* and others. In these stories he depicts simple everyday life. He has a wonderful aptness in describing character, not only that of the principal personages, but in a few brief words he outlines also the minor figures so distinctly that we seem to see them living before us. His style is terse like that of the old sagas. He is as sparing of words as are his heroes. A special charm is given by the lyrics woven into his stories.

Björnson began early to write for the stage. Even older than *Synnöve Solbakken* is his first drama, *Between the Battles.* In extent his dramatic writings far exceeded what he otherwise wrote, but he never mastered the drama to the same degree as the peasant novel. His poems are a delightful collection of lyrics such as is rarely offered to present-day readers. Foremost among them is the wonderful national hymn, "Yes, we love with fond devotion."